2-23-70

A HISTORY OF SEAFARING
THE MERCHANTMEN

Frontispiece Diagrammatic view of *a tea Clipper*

Title page The *Cutty Sark* by Jack Spurling (see pp. 97-8, 115 ff.)

A HISTORY OF SEAFARING

1 Fore Course	8 Lee Fore Topgallant Stun'sail	15 Weather Main Topmast Stun'sail	22 Mizzen Topgallant	29 Main Topmast Staysail
2 Fore Lower Topsail	9 Main Course	16 Weather Main Topgallant Stun'sail	23 Mizzen Royal	30 Mizzen Topgallant Staysail
3 Fore Upper Topsail	10 Main Lower Topsail	17 Lee Main Topgallant Stun'sail	24 Flying Jib	31 Mizzen Topmast Staysail
4 Fore Topgallant	11 Main Upper Topsail	18 Lee Main Topmast Stun'sail	25 Jib	32 Main Spencer
5 Fore Royal	12 Main Topgallant	19 Crossjack	26 Fore Topmast Staysail	33 Spanker
6 Weather Fore Topmast Stun'sail	13 Main Royal	20 Mizzen Lower Topsail	27 Main Royal Staysail	
7 Weather Fore Topgallant Stun'sail	14 Main Skysail	21 Mizzen Upper Topsail	28 Main Topgallant Staysail	

The Merchantmen

BY RICHARD ARMSTRONG

FREDERICK A. PRAEGER, *Publishers*

New York · Washington

BOOKS THAT MATTER

Published in the United States of America in 1969
by Frederick A. Praeger, Inc., Publishers
111 Fourth Avenue, New York, N.Y. 10003

© 1969, in England, by Richard Armstrong

Maps and drawings by Ivan Lapper

Library of Congress Catalog Card Number: 79-79067

Printed in Great Britain

Contents

1530032

Maps

1 Departure of the *Mayflower* from Plymouth. From a painting
by Gustave Alaux

Introduction

SEAFARING AS A WAY OF LIFE has changed more profoundly and comprehensively during the last hundred years than in the whole of its previous history. In this period, the mariner – that restless, roving spirit who had already contributed so much to the emergence of man from the shadows, who was strong precisely because he was footloose and effective because of his individuality – embraced respectability and acquired possessions other than his hard-weather clothes and the tools of his trade. He learned at last to conform, and from then on something in his nature that had distinguished him from other men for thousands of years, began to erode. In one sense it was a good time for him; maybe the best he had ever known; and if he was clever enough, endowed with a personality sufficiently forceful to lift him into command, and could boast the ruthlessness and peculiar courage needed for the fullest exploitation of that dizzy eminence, his life was princely. But only for a little while. Then the organisation-men, the water-clerks, the shore superintendents, the accountants, the experts in market research, and the whole hierarchy of high-powered management, began to close in on him; and that was the end of his freedom. His swan-song was both beautiful and wild, satisfying and fulfilling beyond all belief; but it was quickly over, and soon now, the last of those who can recall it will have passed on, leaving it to become a legend, a heritage ritualised out of all true recognition.

As with the seaman, so also with his ships. They passed through centuries of growth and development so slow it became perceptible only in retrospect; then suddenly there was the incredible flowering, woefully brief, and after it the passing, so total and absolute that it is impossible for men who lived with it to believe it could have happened.

The factors involved in this enormous change are numerous. Some of them are abstractions, the causes of action rather than the action itself. Human folly, for example, and greed as well as the compensatory development of liberal ideas. Others are concrete and measurable with some degree of confidence and certainty. Both categories have been subjected to distortion by national pride and in some cases, maybe, an unrealised collective guilt. So in this as in much else, successive historians have *bent* the record to fit their own peculiar prejudices and allegiances. The slave trade is a case in point and one can still find apologists for this monstrous iniquity even today.

It is the very complexity of these influences – ideas and actions alike – and the way they have interacted on each other that makes this period in the history of seafaring so rich and satisfying a story; for a number of them can be isolated and their effects analysed.

First among them is the natural increase in the number of people on the earth, that process which is so inevitable it has become the current nightmare of rulers and prelates. Thus the population of the known world in Roman times was somewhere in the region of 54 million. By the middle of the 19th century it had increased to 1,300 million and in 1954 it was estimated to be 2,650 million, which means it had doubled itself in just on a hundred years. All these people had to be fed, clothed, and, with a few exceptions, housed; even the most primitive among them ate to live and needed

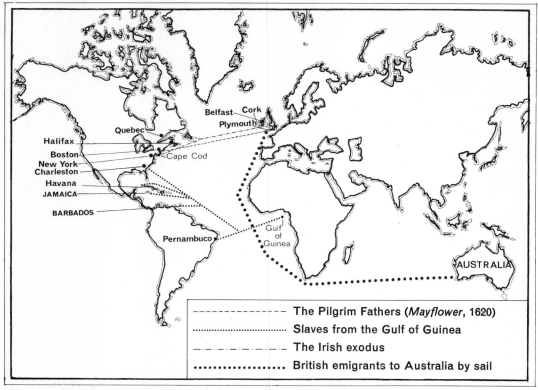

----------- The Pilgrim Fathers (*Mayflower*, 1620)

.... Slaves from the Gulf of Guinea

-·-·-·-·-·-·- The Irish exodus

••••••••••••• British emigrants to Australia by sail

MAP NO. 1   The main streams of migrating people in the 17th,
            18th, and 19th centuries

weapons for hunting or tools for tilling and utensils for the cooking of what food they
were able to win; while the wants of the more sophisticated multiplied faster than their
own numbers. So the earth was forced to produce more and more of an ever-increasing
range of commodities. This demanded machinery, fertilisers, roads, and various forms
of transport to use on them and all these things had to be moved from the producer to
the consumer. Sometimes the transfer was simple and direct; but with the development
of steam-power and machine-tools the manufacturer's intervention became wider and
more comprehensive. Steel was imported as iron ore and other minerals and exported
as railway lines and locomotives; leather came in as raw-hides and went out as shoes;
vegetable fibres from the plantations of America became finished cloth in Lancashire
cotton-mills; and it all added up to a further enormous increase in the total volume of
cargoes for the carriers.

Another powerful factor bearing on the way of life of the seafarer was the large-
scale movement of people which invariably followed wars, religious persecution, political
upheavals, and significant economic changes. Notable among these migrating waves
were the Dutch and English Puritans who founded Pennsylvania and the New England
States and are usually referred to as the Founding Fathers. The Australian gold-rush in
1851 which trebled the population of that vast continent in three years was another; so too
was the exodus from Ireland after England repealed her Corn Laws in 1846, whereby its
population was reduced from 8 million plus in 1841 to well under 5 million 50 years
later in spite of the natural increase. Altogether it is estimated that between 1837 and
1891 at least 30 million people emigrated from Europe; and all that immense concourse
of human beings, with their goods and chattels, were moved by sea.

8

That many of them travelled under conditions of great hardship and extreme squalor is beside the point, which is that it had to be done with the greatest possible speed to ensure the minimum loss of life and the maximum profit for those in the business. It was up to the carriers, and as always they found the means but only at the cost of profound changes in the structure of trade, the size and design of ships, and the methods of running them.

Presumably records of every one of these migrants exist in one form or another – some in government archives, some in shipping lists, others in private correspondence, and possibly most of all in family histories handed down by word of mouth – and given the time it should be possible in theory to break the total figure down into terms of individual hopes and fears; but time on the scale required for such an exercise is not available even to institutions dedicated to that kind of research and to create a mental picture of what this movement of people meant to the seafarer involved in it, one can only go on juggling with figures.

Sailing ships more than doubled their size over the second and third quarters of the 19th century, but the *Alnwick Castle*, built in 1856, might be taken as an example. She was a Blackwall frigate of 1,087 tons and one of the fastest of her kind. Built in Sunderland for Green and Wigram, she was employed in the *coolie trade* – carrying contract labour from Calcutta to the West Indies when the supply of slaves for the plantations had dried up after abolition – and on a typical voyage in 1860 she transported '. . . 225 men, 102 women, 26 boys, 20 girls and 10 infants, from Calcutta to Georgetown . . .' (Lubbock, *The Blackwall Frigates*, p 195). She was 83 days on the passage during which 31 of her passengers died. In the same year, the *Champion of the Seas*, which was a Liverpool ship almost twice the size of the Blackwaller (1,947 tons), carried 403 passengers to Melbourne. Other Liverpool ships making the Australian run that year were:

Prince of the Seas (1,316 tons)	414 passengers
Blue Jacket (1,790 tons)	413 passengers
Red Jacket (1,597 tons)	405 passengers

and no other ship topped the 400. Thus 400 souls per ship per voyage would seem a reasonable maximum for the period and, at that, 30 million emigrants in 50 years

2 The Pilgrim Fathers landing on Plymouth Rock. From a painting by Charles Lucy (1814–73)

9

3   The *Alnwick Castle* (1856), 1,087 tons. A Blackwall frigate in
the coolie trade

breaks down to at least 30 ship-loads a week. When allowances are made for the
difference in the size and capacity of the ships engaged in the traffic and for the enormous variation in the amount of accommodation provided per head, it could amount to
something nearer a hundred.

With passages to the Caribbean taking almost three months and those to the
Antipodes anything up to four, it follows that these migrants exerted extreme pressure
on existing individual ships as well as on shipping in general. Indeed, this aspect of the
developing world alone was dynamic enough for fundamental change. That it did not
create complete chaos and much more suffering can be put down in large measure to
the adaptability of the seafarer and his peculiar genius for coping with what Jack London
once called the *monstrous and inconceivable*.

The effects of the abstract influences are more subtle and much less easy to pin-
point and evaluate. There is always a temptation to over-simplify. For example, the
abolition of slavery is for ever linked with the name of William Wilberforce and the
establishment of a maximum load line for ships with that of Samuel Plimsoll; but both

these reforms and many others like them should really be credited to great upsurges of humanitarianism and liberal thinking. As for the desire of mankind for a richer, fuller life, which is another of the abstractions, this is self-perpetuating, and the demands it makes on seaborne transport for its fulfilment have always been unpredictable.

Greed, however, is a different proposition. There is plenty of it in the history of the seafarer where it has manifested itself in various guises – lust for power, hunger for possessions, dynastic ambition, and plain craving for more and more money. This greed was the dynamic behind the Atlantic slave trade which in the course of 400 years – between 1450 and 1850 – forcibly transported not less than 24 million Africans to the Americas, an operation during which three out of every eight – 9 million in all – died in transit. Greed has shown itself in other ways too – overloading as a deliberate policy, cutting standards of accommodation, evading safety regulations, putting ships into trades for which they were neither designed nor properly equipped, and, above all, cutting down on the quality and quantity of their victualling, an exercise in parsimony which the seaman knows as *belly-robbing* and regards as the ultimate of all the crimes committed against him.

Finally, when all these things have been examined and due allowance has been made for scientific discovery and technological advance, the effect of what is perhaps the most potent factor of all – the inescapable historical process itself – is still unmeasured. It must remain so for this is one thing about which we can only speculate and wonder.

The significant period is the half-century from 1830 to 1880. It was then that the various factors really began to bite; but the writing was on the wall for the seafarer long before that and some of the many threads that make up the story can be followed back to Columbus and Vespucci, even to Henry the Navigator himself. The pattern of development, however, began to establish itself recognisably in the 18th century and the year 1700 is as good a starting-point as any.

4   King Charles II (1660–85) in whose reign the most famous of the Navigation Acts was put on the statute book

The Struggle for Empire

From the early 17th century onward colonisation and trade are
inseparable, and shipping is closely tied to both.
[J. B. Condliffe, *The Commerce of Nations*]

I

IN THE MIDDLE AGES the seafarer's world was centred in the Mediterranean basin
with Venice as the gateway to the East; but the discovery of the route to India via the
Cape of Good Hope and the finding of a whole new world across the Western Ocean,
changed all that. Venice, Genoa, and Florence, after cradling the Renaissance and
initiating the age of discovery, lost their supremacy to Spain and Portugal, while
shipping began to use such northern ports as London and Antwerp which were better
placed geographically for traffic with the Americas. One of the consequences of this
shift was the rise of the Dutch who broke the Portuguese monopoly of trade with the
Spice Islands and eventually took it over almost entirely. This was in the 17th century,
and before the end of it England was at war with Holland, challenging her for control
of seaborne trade.

Long before that, however, carrying itself had been recognised as a lucrative
by-product of commerce and for generations people in power had tried to grab off more
than their fair share of it and even to monopolise it altogether. Sometimes they used the
crudest of strong-arm tactics, wrecking the ships of the opposition and cutting the
throats of their crews or selling them into slavery. But generally speaking, and particularly since the rise of Christianity, men have preferred to pursue their selfish ends
under a cloak of legality and there have been laws in existence restricting the seafarer
in his role as carrier from a long way back.

These laws were called *Navigation Acts* and the earliest English one dates back to
Richard II, though the most famous and troublesome was passed by the Rump of the
Long Parliament in 1651. Standing on the Statute Book as 12 Chas. II, 18 under the
date 1660 and entitled *An Act for the Encouraging and Increasing of Shipping and Navigation*,
it reads:

> For the increase of shipping and encouragement of the navigation of this nation wherein,
> under the good providence and protection of God, the wealth, safety and strength of this
> kingdom is so much concerned; be it enacted by the King's most excellent majesty, and
> by the lords and commons in this present parliament assembled, and by the authority
> thereof, that from and after the first day of December one thousand six hundred and sixty,
> and from thenceforward, no goods or commodities whatsoever shall be imported into or
> exported out of any lands, islands, plantations or territories to his Majesty belonging or in
> his possession, or which may hereafter belong unto or be in the possession of His Majesty,
> his heirs and successors, in Asia, Africa or America, in any other ship or ships, vessel or
> vessels whatsoever, but in such ships or vessels as do truly and without fraud belong
> only to the people of England or Ireland, dominion of Wales or town of Berwick-upon-
> Tweed or are of the build of and belonging to any the said lands, islands, plantations or

territories, as the proprietors and right owners thereof, and whereof the master and three-fourths of the mariners at least are English.

And it is further enacted by the authority aforesaid, that no goods or commodities that are of foreign growth, production or manufacture, and which are brought into England, Ireland, Wales, the Islands of Guernsey and Jersey, or town of Berwick-upon-Tweed, in English-built shipping, or other shipping belonging to some of the aforesaid places, and navigated by English mariners, as aforesaid, shall be shipped or brought from any other place or places, country or countries, but only from those of the said growth, production or manufacture, or from those ports where the said goods and commodities can only, or are, or usually have been first shipped for transportation, and from none other place or countries. [*English Economic History, Select Documents*]

That would seem to sew it all up very neatly for English ships and those who got their living out of running them; but the Navigation Acts, because the very basis of them was restriction, did little good to seafarers and a great deal of harm to other people.

By this time the Dutch had become a very powerful seafaring nation and the number, size, and efficiency of their ships backed by elaborate commercial organisation 'had made Holland a centre for the re-distribution of commodities brought from all over the world' (Morton, *A People's History of England*, p 259). They, like the English, had got their priorities right at a relatively early date and '. . . concentrated upon trade, shipping and colonisation as more profitable than gold-hunting or plunder . . .' (Condliffe, op. cit., p 62). Consequently the two countries were at war for markets and trade routes, raw materials, and a bigger share in the carrying of them long before the end of the 17th century.

Later France became the enemy and these wars between European nations for commercial and maritime supremacy continued down into the mid-19th century and the incidence as well as the overall duration of them is vividly expressed by Schlote:

5   A Dutch ship entering an Italian port. A painting by Cornelis Bouwmaester (*c.* 1670–1733)

6   The Seven Years War in Europe, November 1757. Frederick
the Great of Prussia at the battle of Rossbach, where his army
won a great victory over the armies of France and the Empire

> Between 1697 and 1783 there were forty-five years of peace and forty-two years of war.
> Between 1697 and 1815 there were fifty-five years of peace and sixty-four years of war....
> [*British Overseas Trade*, p 41 n]

The conflicts were invariably wrapped up in some high-toned abstraction or moral principle; and most important among them were the War of the League of Augsburg (1689–97), aimed at crippling France; the War of the Spanish Succession (1701–13), which gave England a monopoly of the slave trade with the Spanish colonies in the New World; the Seven Years War (1756–63), again against France for the control of India, North America, and the West Indies; the American War of Independence (1774–83); and finally the Napoleonic Wars (1793–1815), which gave English shipping the bulge for almost a hundred years.

   The following figures extracted from a table in Schlote's *British Overseas Trade* illustrate with remarkable clarity the effects of this long struggle on British trade and shipping:

	Br. Imports from Europe	Br. Imports from America	Br. Exports to Europe	Br. Exports to America
1701	64·8%	19·6%	80·8%	11·9%
1801–2	32·7%	45·4%	55·2%	33·5%

The shift of emphasis is marked.

   There has always been a tendency to look for the glamour and romance of this period in the eastern trade, but Condliffe at least is in no doubt about which mattered most in the long run to the seafarer in particular and mankind in general:

> Important as was this imperial expansion [in India] it was less important for the future of international trade than the steady growth of settlement in the North American colonies. . . . Colonial policy, in the strict sense of the word, was based upon the ideas of

nationalism then current. A mixture of motives operated. The desirability of securing assured access to strategic raw materials loomed large. New outlets for manufactured goods and enlargement of the carrying trade were important also. . . .   [op. cit., p 81]

The English were clearer sighted about this than the French, or maybe just a little bit more shrewd, for although France had established colonies along the banks of the St Lawrence River as early as 1608, they got hung up on the fur trade. This was no doubt extremely rewarding at the time, but it did nothing towards the development of the settlements. Consequently, at the outbreak of the Seven Years War there were still only some 60,000 colonists in the French territories against something like 2 million in the English ones. It was people with their roots established who mattered in the end.

Nevertheless, life for the colonists was anything but a bed of roses. They were squeezed to the limit and their own trade hedged in by all manner of restrictions imposed by the government at home. Morton is quite specific about the reasons:

The economic organisation of the Empire in the Eighteenth Century, embodied in the Navigation Acts [he says], had as its object the utilisation of the trade and wealth of the colonies for the exclusive benefit of the English ruling class. The most valuable products of the colonies, the tobacco of Virginia, the rice of the Carolinas, the sugar of the West Indies and the tar and timber of New England, priceless material for naval construction, might only be exported to England or Scotland. . . . Equally, the colonies were forbidden to import manufactured goods from any foreign country and the development of colonial industry was checked where it might endanger home industry. Thus, although the smelting of iron reached some importance in New England early in the Eighteenth Century, the manufacture of iron and steel goods there was prohibited and the raw iron had to be shipped across the Atlantic to England, from which the Americans had to import manufactured iron goods for their own use. . . .   [op. cit., p 304]

MAP NO. 2   Trade routes of the Chartered Companies (1600–1800)

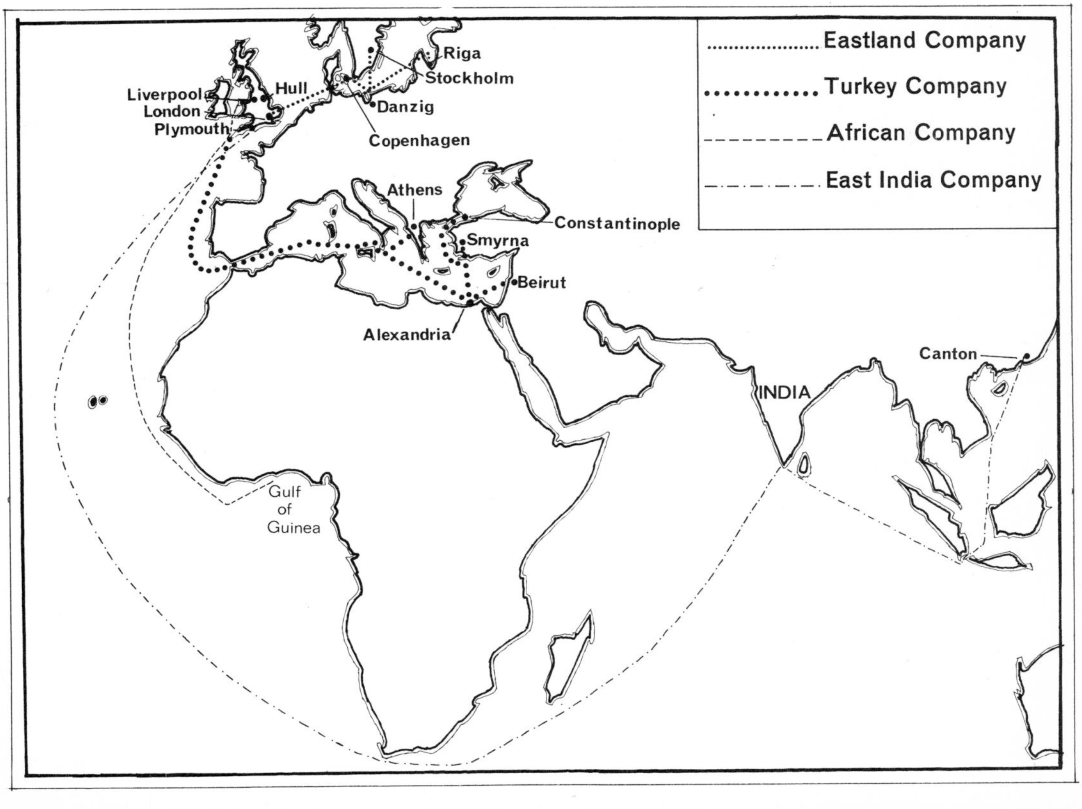

The dominant influence on trade and consequently on shipping and the seafarer in this period was that of the *chartered companies*. These were a peculiarly English institution dating from medieval times, when the monarch granted to associated groups of individuals the exclusive right to trade in specified areas. There was always *a consideration* involved and in the first place the charter was probably no more than a bright idea for replenishing the royal purse. But it caught on. In the 15th century, for example, a Company of Merchant Adventurers was formed to export cloth to northern Europe; and a hundred years later the chartered companies in existence included the Eastland Company, which ran the Baltic trade; the Turkey Company, with a monopoly in the Levant; and the African Company, formed expressly to organise the slave trade. The biggest of all and the longest lived was the East India Company, which was founded in 1600, had wrested control of India from the Portuguese by 1614, established bases at Calcutta and Madras a few years later, seriously challenged the Dutch monopoly of the spice trade, and for two centuries not only ruled the whole sub-continent of India, but also dominated the seafarer's world in the East.

The East India Company's first venture was made in 1601. It consisted of a fleet of five ships under the command of Sir James Lancaster who had already made the voyage via the Cape nine years before. All five ships returned with 'a rich cargo of spices' and earned 'a substantial profit for the Company'.

H. B. Morse, in *The Chronicles of the East India Company trading to China 1635–1834*, gives the official title of the concern as *The United Company of Merchants of England Trading to the East Indies* and provides an almost inexhaustible collection of facts and figures about its business. For instance:

The beginnings of the English Company were modest. In its first nineteen years, 1601–20, its export trade to the East Indies was of the following value:

	Total	Annual average
Woollens, metals, and other English products	£292,286	£15,383
Silver bullion and coin	548,090	28,847
	£840,376	£44,230

In the single year 1674–5 the whole trade was of the following value:

Export: Woollens, metals &c.:		
Company's trade	£110,000	
Private trade of officers	45,000	£155,000
Silver bullion and coin:		
Company's trade	320,000	
Private trade of officers	90,000	410,000
		£565,000
Import: Cotton cloth, saltpetre, indigo, silks, pepper, spices, &c.		£860,000

[vol. 1, p 8]

This gives some idea of the rate at which the Company's business was expanding.

The trade continued to expand and in the 50 years between 1710 and 1759 the export side of it came to 'a total of £9,248,306 in goods, and £26,833,614 in bullion and coin, an annual average of £184,966 and £536,672 respectively . . .' (ibid).

In the early days of the Company's existence, Chinese products could only be bought by them in India or at best in the ports of the Malay Archipelago. The case of tea is typical. It could only be obtained from China, and Morse has the following to say about its beginnings in the carrying trade:

> The first notice taken of the leaf in England was in 1664, when 2 lb. 2 oz. were bought by the Directors of the Company at a cost of £4 5s. to be presented to His Majesty, and again in 1666, when 22 lb. 12 oz. were bought for £56 17s. 6d.; these lots of tea came, presumably, from Holland, or, possibly, were bought from their own ship's officers. The first importation made by the Company appears to have been in 1669, when 143 lb. were received; then 79 lb. in 1670; both from Bantam. Thereafter tea was imported year by year, from Bantam, from Surat, from Ganjam, from Madras, until 1689, in which year there is the first record of an importation of tea from Amoy. One of the importations from Bantam is noted as having been 'part of the present from Tywan,' but in general the Company's factors bought, at Bantam from Chinese junks trading there and at Surat from the Portuguese ships trading from Macao to Goa and Daman. Nearer than this they could not get in reaching out for the China trade.   [ibid., p 9]

Nevertheless, the Company had a ship – the *Hinde* – looking for a cargo in Macao in 1644 and it is recorded that in 1671 they sent out three ships – the *Experiment*, the *Return*, and the *Zant* frigate – with orders to push beyond Bantam and open up trade with Taiwan (Formosa), Japan, and Tonking. The *Zant*'s outward cargo, or *stock* as it was more usually called, is listed as follows:

53 bales of cloth	159 piculs of sandalwood
257 piculs of lead	38 bales of drugs (medicinal plants)
10 great guns	8 packages of sundries
16 chests of brimstone	10,000 Reals of eight
618 piculs of pepper	[ibid., p 37]

7   September 1759. British soldiers, commanded by General James Wolfe, sail up the St Lawrence, land, and scale the heights of Quebec. The battle of Quebec was a decisive British victory of the Seven Years War

8 Silver coins used by the H.E.I. Co. in the China trade: *top left and bottom*, Piece of Eight (1691); *top right*, Pillar dollar (1733)

Morse, with commendable thoroughness, provides a table of equivalents which might well be quoted here:

Currency: The tael of currency at Canton was treated in the accounts as equivalent to 6*s.* 8*d.* (£1 = Tls. 3).

The Spanish dollar was treated in the accounts as equivalent to Tls. 0·72, the exact equivalence in weight (apart from the touch of the silver) being Tls. 100 = 120·8 oz. troy.

The Spanish dollar was invoiced from 1619 to 1814 at 5*s.* per dollar (£1 = 4 dollars). From 1815 it was invoiced at the actual cost (c.i.f.) per oz. Salaries and other fixed charges at Canton were paid at the rate £100 = $416·67. Bills on the Company in London were issued at rates ranging from 4*s.* 10*d.* to 6*s.* per dollar, for bills payable 365 days after sight.

Weight: The picul is 133⅓ lb. av. = 100 catties.
The catty is 1⅓ lb. av. = 16 taels.
The tael is 1⅓ oz. av.
The tael of Canton was actually 579·85 grains.

Length: The *ch'ih* or 'covid' or 'cubit' of the carpenters of Canton was 14·1 English inches; used for measuring ships and cloth.

Reverting to the breakdown of the total export figures on pp 14-16, note should be taken of the large amounts of bullion and coin regularly shipped to the Orient, particularly in relation to the total value of goods in the same cargoes. This is largely explained by the fact that in those days there were no banks of exchange and shipowners had no established commercial organisation in the outports. The seafarer, once he had dropped his pilot, was well and truly out on his own and when he had worked his ship to her destination, he, or his supercargo, became his own broker and agent with sole responsibility for selling his 'stock' and buying his homeward cargo on the best terms he could make. But the navigation laws current in the 18th century demanded that not less than one-tenth of a ship's cargo outward from England should consist of goods or commodities which were 'the growth, produce or manufacture of the Kingdom;' and

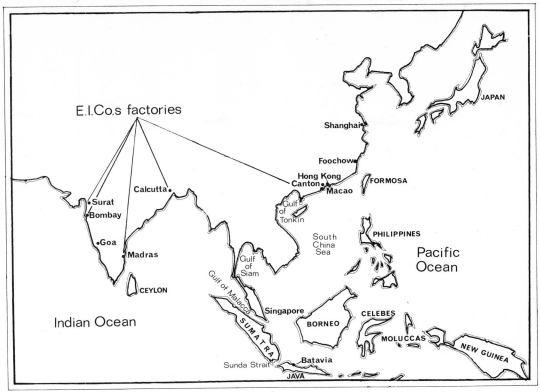

MAP NO. 3   East India Company's factories and ports of call in India and China

by one of those curious inversions created by custom, or maybe just because a thing as volatile and unpredictable as trade cannot be tied down, this eventually created a situation wherein that tenth became the maximum proportion of English goods any ship could get rid of in China, from an outward cargo.

On this point Morse says:

> Lead was 'as good as money' and each ship took usually from 40 to 60 tons of it; woollen goods were sold with difficulty, without profit, and in small quantities; and China asked for nothing else that was English. Sometimes, but less often as time went on, ships from England went, on the way out, to Sumatra . . . or to Borneo . . . and loaded from 50 to 100 tons of pepper for sale in China. Generally speaking, however, at the period we are now describing nine-tenths of each ship's stock consisted of silver sent from England.
>
> [ibid., pp 67–8]

A feature of the traffic was the variety of currency used in it. It was forbidden by law to take English silver coins out of the country, and though some silver was shipped in bars most of it was in coin minted elsewhere, in Europe or the Americas. So any ship eastward bound would be carrying some or all of the following kinds of money:

> Pillar dollars, ryals of eight, pieces of eight: minted at the Royal Mint of Seville; current in the China trade for three centuries; 95 touch, of the Chinese standard.
> Mexico dollars: minted at the Viceroyal Mint of Mexico; from 1855 the ordinary currency of the treaty ports of South China; 94 touch.
> Duccatoons: minted by the Mint of Venice; 96 touch.
> French crowns: minted by the Royal Mints of France; 95 touch if bearing three crowns on reverse, otherwise 93 or 92 touch.
> Rixdollars: not stated if from Scandinavian or German mints; 90 touch.   [ibid.]

Touch was the method of defining the quality of the silver in the coins; i.e. the higher the touch the finer the metal. They were shipped in chests which carried a standardised net load of 290 lbs. 8 oz. troy and took about 4,000 coins each.

The East India Company is reputed to have been the most liberal and open-handed employer the seafaring man has ever encountered, and there is no doubt whatsoever that it was under the Company's red and white striped house-flag that, for masters and officers anyhow, the life was at its richest and the material rewards it paid at their peak. Yet the wages of its staff both ashore and afloat were ridiculously low. The chief of the Company's factory (or depot) at Amoy in 1681 had a salary of £80 a year, junior officials received £40 a year, and writers (young men of good family out from England to learn the business) got only £10 a year. So too with the seamen. Even as late as 1813, in which year the Company lost its monopoly, it was paying its masters a mere £10 a month. What made the job so much sought after was the peculiar system of *privileges*. In the first place, the supercargo and the ship's people in general were allowed to do a certain amount of trading on their own account, and one instance of the scope of this item is shown in the table on p 16. Morse gives another in the case of the ship *Eaton*, which was chartered by the Company for China in 1699:

> '*Private Trade:* The Court have allowed by the Charter-party £3500 to be sent out by the Owners, Master and Ship's Company of the *Eaton*; whereof £1500 may be carried out and brought home in such Commodities as they please, on condition that her Captain do not sell or buy in China without the Concurrence of the Factory. The remaining £2000 is [to be] sent out in Silver; and the Court permit the proceeds to be returned from China in Gold, or otherwise may be sent to Coromandel, consigned to some of the Company's Factors to be returned thence in Diamonds by a Company's Ship, the Proprietors paying what others pay.' [ibid., p 73]

Again in 1714 it is recorded that ships' captains and officers brought into the country on their own trading accounts a total of 20,000 lbs. of tea. Soon after that, however, the Company began to be worried about the effect of this private trade on their own business, and in 1720 the rules were altered to limit it. After that date the private trade on any voyage was not to exceed 3 per cent of the ship's tonnage, and it was later cut again to 2 cwt. (224 lbs.) for every 100 tons of the ship's tonnage. The Company's main concern was to stop the *privilege* encroaching on actual cargo space and a man could do what he liked with his own cabin. Consequently, the emphasis of the private trade gradually shifted from commodities like tea to things like fans, ivory carvings, and other curios. Nevertheless, the rules were often bent to fit special people and circumstances and

> . . . in 1729 we find the captain of the ship *Lynn* having private trade from Canton valued at £3,744, being £2,500 in gold and £1,244 in goods, including 7,750 lb. of tea. . . . [ibid.]

A hundred years later they were doing even better and Basil Lubbock in *The Blackwall Frigates* quotes a claim for compensation made against the Company by a Captain Innes of the *Abercrombie Robinson* in which he estimates the average income from his last three voyages, *exclusive of profits or investments*, as £6,100 per voyage, made up as follows:

Eighteen months' pay at £10 per month	£180
56 tons privilege outward at £4 per ton	224
From port to port at 30 rupees per candy	336
Homeward at £33 per ton	1,848

Two-fifths tonnage from port to port, 478 tons at 30 rupees
    per candy, less charged by the Hon. Coy £2 per ton   £1,912

Primage   100

Passage money after allowing for the provisions and stores
    provided for the passengers   1,500

                         Total £6,100

[p 53]

Another commander is said to have made a total of £30,000 out of one single voyage from London to India, then to China and back home – and £8,000 to £10,000 a voyage was reckoned to be the usual thing.

On top of the pay the ship's people, including master and supercargo, were all-found and the provisioning was lavish. Among the extras allowed to the chief officer, for example, was 1 cwt. of cheese, 2 firkins of butter, 4 quarter cases of pickles, and 1 cwt. of grocery; he also had 24 dozen of wine or beer and a puncheon of rum for the ward-room. The master's allowance of liquor was fantastic, the ceiling for him being 11 tons of wine, beer, and other liquors with two pipes of Madeira wine thrown in. Then the captain had two personal servants and the chief officer, second officer, surgeon, bosun, gunner, and carpenter, one each. 'No wonder,' says Lubbock, 'that the Merchant Service was sought after by the highest in the land.'

The system of low salaries and high privileges had its drawbacks and chief among them was the way it encouraged corruption. This spread like a disease throughout the territories in which the Company operated.

It was the practice of the Company to pay its servants only a nominal wage: their real, and in the higher grades vast, incomes were derived from bribes, extortion and private trade . . . Even the Directors of the Company were forced to condemn a system which they themselves had created and which finally threatened the profits of the shareholders. They complained of the 'deplorable state to which our affairs are on the point of being reduced, from the corruption and rapacity of our servants, and the universal depravity of manners throughout the settlement. . . . We must add that we think the vast fortunes, acquired in the inland trade, had been obtained by a series of the most tyrannic and oppressive conduct that was ever known in any country.'   [Morton, op. cit., p 296]

In spite of all its folly, the evils perpetrated in its name, and fierce competition from the French, the East India Company continued to grow throughout the 18th century. By 1740 its capital had risen to £3 million on which it was paying a dividend of 7 per cent. This was chicken-feed, however, compared with the real profit, the enormity of which can only be inferred and never even approximately calculated. One of the known facts that underlines the immensity of the fortunes made is that in ten years from 1757 to 1766 the Company and its servants extorted over £6 million in bribes from the State of Bengal alone and the same sort of thing on a similar scale was going on in Madras and the Carnatic, and wherever else the Company's writ ran.

But the concern here is with the East India Company's ships, the seamen who ran them, and the cargoes they carried. The ships were not usually owned by the Company but chartered – *taken up* was the term used – for one or more voyages. The owner was referred to as a *ship's husband* or, in the case of those chartering their ships to the Company, an *India husband*. This custom adds to the obscurity surrounding the huge fortunes made in the eastern trade because the owners were usually big shareholders in the East India Company and the whole business constituted a monopoly run by a tight ring of extremely rich men into which the outsider could neither worm nor blast his way. To add to the confusion a little, the ships were invariably built for the trade and 'conformed in every particular of design and building material to the rules and regulations laid down by the Company' (Lubbock, op. cit., p 42). As to size, Morse notes that:

> . . . Up to 1753 they were under 500 tons burthen, in the last years preceding that of a uniform tonnage of 498 – the reason being that, up to 1772, the Company was by its charter required to carry a chaplain on each ship of or exceeding 500 tons . . .
>
> [op. cit., vol II, p 11]

and such dead-heads as parsons, of course, besides costing good money in stipend and provisions, occupied space that could be more profitably used for cargo.

It is interesting to note at this point that in spite of all its power the Company never achieved a complete monopoly of the China trade. In 1784, for example, the ships loading in Canton were: English, 21; French, 4; Dutch, 4; Danish, 4; American, 1. That American was the first ever of that nationality on the coast. She was the *Empress of China* (360 tons; Captain John Green), and she came from New York. Her cargo inward was:

Cotton, 316 piculs, realized	Tls. 3,160
Lead, 476 piculs, realized	1,904
Pepper, 26 piculs, realized	260
Camlets, 1270 pieces, realized	45,720
Skins (furs), 2,600 pieces, realized	5,000 estimated.
Ginseng, 473 piculs, realized	80,410
	Tls. 136,454

Outward from Canton she took:

Tea, black, 2,460 piculs, cost	Tls. 49,240
Tea, green, 562 piculs, cost	16,860
Nankeens, 24 piculs (864 pieces)	362
Chinaware, 962 piculs, cost	2,500
Woven silk, 490 pieces, cost	2,500
Cassia, 21 piculs, cost	305
	Tls. 71,767

[ibid., p 95]

Twenty years later – in 1803 – 23 American ships loaded in Canton, 11 of them coming from Atlantic ports direct, while '. . . 6 were from Pacific ports of the North American continent, 5 were from ports of call in the "South Seas," and one was from Havre de Grace' (ibid., p 401).

The Company were as prodigal with time as they were with *privilege*, and 14 to 15 months were allowed for the two passages out and home, with another 6 months for discharging and loading. The timing of arrivals and sailings was dictated by the monsoon, the aim being to complete on the coast and sail for home while the north-east monsoon was still blowing strong enough to bring the ship in reasonably fast time down to the Straits of Sunda. Often enough something went wrong and Morse records: 'The

Macclesfield, having lost her monsoon, left Canton for "Chusan, the Port of Lingpo" on July 18, 1700' (ibid., vol I, p 97). She finally got away from Chusan on 24 December of that year and arrived off Portsmouth on 1 July 1701 'with a rich and full cargo' after a voyage which had lasted two years and three months. On the outward leg she took 5 months and 24 days to Macao via Batavia.

Long before the end of the 18th century the Company had built up an enviable reputation for honest dealing; so much so that its word on anything was accepted without question in China where it had become known as *The Honourable John Company*. Yet its attitude to the illegal opium trade was curiously ambivalent. The traffic was started by the Portuguese in 1700 when they began importing about 200 chests a year into Macao from India, and the first Chinese edict against it was made in 1729. Thirty years later the annual import was estimated to be 1,000 chests and worth anything up to $2 million. At this time, according to Lubbock, the Company

> . . . countenanced the trade, but as the drug was contraband in China the Court of Directors considered it beneath the dignity of the Company to smuggle and would not allow their Indiamen to carry opium. [*The Opium Clippers*, p 30]

Nevertheless, in 1781 Warren Hastings, then Governor-General of Bengal and head of the Company in the East, finding himself desperately short of ready money, went into opium in a big way. Altogether he shipped on the Company's account

> . . . 1,466 chests on the sloop *Betsy*, invoiced at current rupees 719,108; and 1,601 chests on Lieut.-Colonel Henry Watson's private ship of war *Nonsuch* invoiced at current rupees 825,023. . . . [Morse, op. cit., vol II, p 76]

9 The trial of Warren Hastings in Westminster Hall for corruption and cruelty in his Indian administration was spread over the years 1788–95 and cost him £70,000. He was acquitted

Whether that opened the way or not it is impossible to say, but the trade went on and by the turn of the century the Hon. John Coy were deeply involved in it, though the actual buying and selling in Chinese waters was done by brokers and the pretence of non-involvement which deceived no one was preserved. The situation is vividly illustrated by the following letter: ˙

> The Hong Merchants to the Select Committee of the Honourable East India Company.
> Gentlemen,
>
> We approach to state that opium is a commodity which the laws have heretofore prohibited most strictly, and we have before respectfully received commands to order all the respective ships that they must not bring it.
>
> It has occurred not a second nor a third time only.
>
> Last year Captain Hogg's ship (the *Eugenia*), Captain Robson's (*Hooghley*), Captain Parkyns' (*Merope*), and Captain Coupland's (American ship *Emily*) all brought opium into the port; and these, when it was discovered, were in obedience to the Imperial will, sent away and not allowed to trade; and it was decided that afterwards, if any opium were smuggled into the port, the implicated ship was to be treated in the same manner.
>
> We will trouble the Chief and Committee (of the H.E.I.C.) to send a letter to the Company and to India and to the Marts, informing everyone that opium must not be smuggled into Canton, for if, reverently, orders be received to search and discovery ensue, the ship will be rejected and not allowed to trade; and if this year any ship, not knowing the prohibition, should bring opium, we beg you to inform her that she must not on any account enter the Port, but set sail immediately, for if she do enter and we find it out, we positively cannot become security, but must assuredly and immediately report it to the Great Office of Government that the affair may be prosecuted according to law. This is an affair which concerns our persons, families and lives, and we are compelled to proceed in the straight road of management.
>
> We hope you will excuse us and with Compts, we remain
>
> 2nd Moon 12th day.   Signed by the Hong Merchants.
> March 6th 1822.
>
> [quoted Lubbock, *The Opium Clippers*, pp 53–4]

The trade, however, was much too lucrative to be stopped merely because it put a few lives at risk, and as shall be seen, in the end it took two minor but quite bloody wars to stop it.

In spite of the fortunes to be made in the handling of it, opium remained very much a side-line. The eastern trade was being built up on broader, long-term needs. Prominent among them was tea. The 79 lbs. shipped home from Bantam in 1670 had become a total of 10,619,000 lbs. by 1770 and that in British ships alone. That same year ships of other nationalities brought to Europe in addition just under 20 million lbs. And presently this relatively harmless commodity was also to be the immediate cause of much blood-letting.

══════▷ 3 ◁══════

For 500 years and more the wealth of the East – India, the Spice Islands, and China – has been proverbial, one of those legends handed down from generation to generation with the language and believed in as an irrefutable fact of life. And there is no question about it; such vast land masses, blessed by tropical and sub-tropical climates and occupied by such multitudes of people, could not be otherwise than potentially rich; or, if skilfully exploited and developed, fail to produce immense wealth. But the East has always been glamorised and never more so than during the seafarer's heyday. 'Ship me somewhere's east of Suez . . .', sang Kipling, and he was only one of many. Consequently, the glitter has obscured some rather startling facts about commerce and shipping in the popular mind. One of them is that the West Indies trade was always a better bet than the East, both in terms of capital invested and volume and value of commodities shipped both ways. This was never more so than in the 18th century:

> The West Indies were, indeed, the most profitable of British possessions. In 1790 it was calculated that £70,000,000 was invested there against £18,000,000 in the Far East and that their trade with England was almost double the imports and exports of the East India Company. . . . [Morton, op. cit., pp 311–12]

The validity of this assertion is established by the official returns of numbers and destinations of ships clearing outward from British ports in the year 1806. The total sailing for the British West Indies was 652 and that for the East Indies a mere 63 (J. Holland Rose, *Man and the Sea*, p 227).

The vast wealth of the West Indies was created by the labour, the sweat, and the blood of African slaves; and conditions on the plantations were such that a slave's useful life was short. They were worked to death and the need for constant replacements, coupled with the demand for an ever-expanding labour force, was the imperative behind what came to be known to seafarers as the *Triangular Trade*.

Although an Act prohibiting the slave trade was passed by a British government in 1807, it was not until 1834 that slavery was abolished in the West Indian colonial possessions and in this connection Morton writes:

> Profitable as the slave trade proved during the Eighteenth Century, its suppression in the Nineteenth Century was even more profitable. While slaves were the only important export from West Africa, no attempts were made to penetrate the interior. Instead, the coast tribes were armed and encouraged to raid inland and bring their captives to some half a dozen trading ports for sale and shipment. . . . The planters [in the West Indies] received £20,000,000 in compensation for the loss of their slaves. . . . By a curious irony, the abolition of slavery here stimulated the African slave trade, because the production of sugar in Cuba and Brazil, where slavery still continued, developed rapidly and created a new demand for labour. [ibid., p 467]

The trade was started by the Portuguese in 1441 when a seaman called Gonçalvez took ten Africans home from the Guinea Coast and presented them to Henry the Navigator. There was no question of profit in this transaction. The Africans were hunted down like wild animals and given to the Christian prince in the same way 'that rare plants, exotic butterflies or tropical birds' might have been. Three years later a batch of 235 African men, women, and children were landed in the Portuguese harbour of Lagos and the trade in human flesh and blood that was to last for 400 years was established. The base for it – the great castle at Elmina – was built in 1481 and 'in 1518 Charles V. granted to the Governor of Bresa the monopoly of shipping four thousand African slaves a year to the West Indies' (James Pope-Hennessy, *Sins of the Fathers*, p 8), by which time all pretence at saving the Africans from barbarism had been abandoned. The English were involved in the trade at a very early date, in the person of Sir John Hawkins, who made the first of his three famous voyages in 1562. Hakluyt's account of it, though brief, is extremely illuminating, particularly by implication, and well worth quoting in full:

25

10   The Slave Market. A painting by A. F. Biard

Master John Haukins [he writes] having made divers voyages to the Iles of the Canaries, and there by his good and upright dealing being growen in love and favour with the people, informed himselfe amongst them by diligent inquisition, of the state of the West India, whereof hee had received some knowledge by the instructions of his father, but increased the same by the advertisments and reports of that people. And being amongst other particulars assured, that Negros were very good marchandise in Hispaniola, and that store of Negros might easily bee had upon the coast of Guinea, resolved with himselfe to make triall thereof, and communicated that devise with his worshipfull friendes of London: namely with Sir Lionell Ducket, sir Thomas Lodge, M. Gunson his father in law, sir William Winter, M. Bromfield, and others. All which persons liked so well of his intention, that they became liberall contributors and adventurers in the action. For which purpose there were three good ships immediatly provided: The one called the *Salomon* of the burthen of 120. tunne, wherein M. Haukins himselfe went as Generall: The second the *Swallow* of 100. tunnes, wherein went for Captaine M. Thomas Hampton: and the third the *Jonas* a barke of 40. tunnes, wherein the Master supplied the Captaines roome: in which small fleete M. Hawkins tooke with him not above 100. men for feare of sicknesse and other inconveniences, whereunto men in long voyages are commonly subject.

With this companie he put off and departed from the coast of England in the moneth of October 1562. and in his course touched first at Teneriffe, where hee received friendly intertainement. From thence he passed to Sierra Leona, upon the coast of Guinea, which place by the people of the countrey is called Tagarin, where he stayed some good time, and got into his possession, partly by the sworde, and partly by other meanes, to the number of 300. Negros at the least, besides other merchandises which that countrey yeeldeth. With this praye hee sayled over the Ocean sea unto the Iland of Hispaniola, and arrived first at the port of Isabella: and there hee had reasonable utterance of his English commodities, as also of some part of his Negros, trusting the Spaniards no further, then that by his owne strength he was able still to master them. From the port of Isabella he went to Puerto de Plata, where he made like sales, standing alwaies upon his guard: from thence also hee sayled to Monte Christi another port on the North side of Hispaniola, and the last place of his touching, where he had peaceable traffique, and made vent of the whole number of his Negros: for which he received in those 3. places by way of exchange such quantitie of merchandise, that hee did not onely lade his owne 3. shippes with hides, ginger, sugars, and some quantitie of pearles, but he fraighted also two other hulkes with hides and other like commodities, which hee sent into Spaine. And thus leaving the Iland, he returned and disemboqued, passing out by the Ilands of the Caycos, without further entring into the Bay of Mexico, in this his first voyage to the West India. And so with prosperous success and much gaine to himselfe and the aforesayde adventurers, he came home, and arrived in the moneth of September 1563. [Hakluyt, *Voyages*, vol 7, pp 5–6]

That was the beginning of the Triangular Trade, and by the middle of the 18th century it was being exploited by shipowners all over Europe and slavers were sailing out of London, Lisbon, Liverpool, Amsterdam, Bristol, Nantes, and Copenhagen to name just a few of the principal ports.

As Hakluyt's terse narrative shows, the Triangular Trade had three legs. The first one took the ship concerned from its northern European home port to the Guinea Coast of Africa with a cargo of 'trade goods'. In the early days most of this stuff was trash, but as time went on the African traders learned to be more choosey. A French historian and trader, Jean Barbot, is quoted by Pope-Hennessy as having written in 1682:

The blacks of the Gold Coast are very skilled in the nature and proper qualities of all the Europeans' wares and merchandise vended there; but in a more particular manner, since they have so often been imposed upon by the Europeans, who in former ages made no scruple to cheat them in the qualities, weight and measure of their goods; which at first they received upon content, because they say it could never enter into their thoughts that white men, as they call the Europeans, were so base as to abuse their credulity and good opinion of us. [op. cit., p 15]

MAP NO. 4　The Triangular Trade

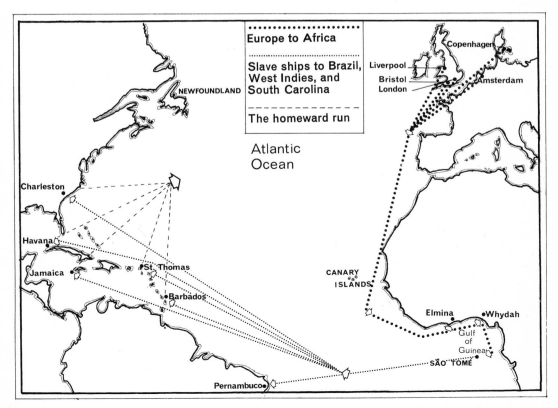

Even so, trade goods for the Guinea Coast continued to be a peculiar assortment of low-grade merchandise. Included in the list were iron bars, brassware, bright coloured cotton and woollen clothes, silks, taffetas, cast-off clothing, cocked hats, and kitchen utensils. Firearms, gun-flints, and gunpowder were in great demand; so were cheap brandy and rum, glass beads, and cowrie shells. This last item originated in the Maldive Islands, where they were gathered among the rocks and shoals, and shipped as ballast to Goa, Cochin, and other ports, eventually arriving in Europe to be packed into small barrels for the Guinea trade. The shells varied in size and the smaller they were the higher their value when used as currency. They were milk-white and looked rather like olives. On the Coast they were bored and threaded on strings in groups of 40, and among certain tribes were prized more than gold-dust, 'a man's rank and power being measured by the number of cowries and the number of domestic slaves he possessed'.

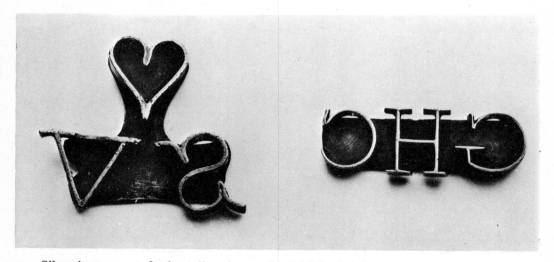

11   Silver instruments for branding slaves with initials of their owners

Pope-Hennessy lays responsibility for developing the trade firmly where it belongs:

> It was the European traders [he says] who assiduously taught Africans to sell other Africans; and, moreover, taught them to sell slaves, as they taught them to sell gold and ivory, for trash. In so far as they studied African psychology at all, the white traders studied it from a shifty street hawker's point of view. Peddling their wares with deftness and contempt, they created an artificial market for cheap brassware and old clothes, faulty iron bars, cottons, gewgaws and aged flintlocks that frequently blew up on use. . . .
> [ibid., p 176]

Some of the slaving ships were known in the trade as *rum vessels*. These usually hailed from New England and carried nothing but rum distilled there from West Indian molasses expressly for the Guinea Coast. On this Pope-Hennessy is again outspoken:

> All slaving ships carried a certain quantity of rum to Africa, since it was important to spread alcoholism on the coast, drunken traders being easier to fox. . . .   [ibid., p. 16n]

If the Africans were careful to see that 'the knives were not rusty, the kettles and basins not cracked, . . . the brandy and rum . . . not adulterated with fresh, or sea, water . . .', the slave-ship masters matched their caution when it came to evaluating the slaves offered. Every one of them, irrespective of age or sex, was submitted to the most humiliating medical examination imaginable, as a check on age and strength and to make sure he or she was not suffering from any kind of disease. Then they were branded with a red-hot iron to prevent any switching.

> This was, of course, the preliminary or traders' branding. On arrival in the transatlantic plantations, the slaves were branded a second time with their new owners' initials. The Society for the Propagation of the Gospel in Foreign Parts, which had inherited two plantations from Christopher Codrington in 1710, would brand their slaves, for instance, with the initials S.P.G.   [ibid., p 78 n]

Once on board, the slaves were treated exactly as any other rather awkward cargo might have been. There was a bare 5 feet of headroom between the decks and this space was divided horizontally by a wooden shelf; so the slaves, chained together in pairs by this time, could be stowed in two tiers. John Newton, who served aboard a slaver and made five voyages to the Guinea Coast, describes in *Thoughts upon the African Slave Trade* how they were laid

> . . . in two rows one above the other, on each side of the ship, close to each other, like books upon a shelf. I have known them so close that the shelf would not easily contain one more. And I have known a white man sent down among the men to lay them in these rows to the greatest advantage, so that as little space as possible be lost. . . . And every morning perhaps more instances than one are found of the living and the dead, like the captives of Mezentius, fastened together.   [quoted Pope-Hennessy, op. cit., p 3]

This then was the freight for the second leg of the triangle – the middle passage across the Atlantic. The conditions under which it was made were not only hard and difficult but beastly and few honest-to-God seafaring men would have anything to do with the trade. A notorious Liverpool slave-ship captain writing in 1830 described the crews as 'the very dregs of the community'. Many were criminals, jail-breakers on the run, and well-bred sons of gentlemen dodging their creditors or fleeing from some unnameable folly; and the Guinea Coast did nothing to regenerate them. They rotted and drank themselves to an early death in the effort to forget the stench of what they were involved in.

As an example of that second leg, a voyage of the slave-ship *Hannibal* (Captain Thomas Phillips) might be quoted. She was a ship of 450 tons, armed with 36 guns, and she sailed from the Downs in October 1693. On the Guinea Coast, Phillips purchased (by trade) 700 negroes and 12 of them were dead before the passage began, having committed suicide by jumping overboard off the port of Whydah rather than face the hell of slavery. Captain Phillips left a journal in which he recorded:

> We spent in our passage from St. Thomas [São Tomé] to Barbados two months eleven days . . . in which time there happened much sickness and mortality among my poor men and negroes, that of the first we buried 14, and of the last 320 . . . whereby the loss in all amounted to near 6560 pounds sterling. The distemper which my men as well as the blacks mostly die of, was the white flux, which was so violent and inveterate, that no medicine would in the least check it; so that when any of our men were seized with it, we esteemed him a dead man as he generally proved.   [quoted Pope-Hennessy, op. cit., p. 97]

The slaves were brought up on deck twice a day to be fed – at ten in the morning and four in the afternoon, and to discourage any thoughts of revolt, the ship's big guns were trained on them and all hands stood to arms while they ate. Alexander Falconbridge, who made many voyages as doctor on board slave-ships, published *An Account of the Slave Trade* in 1788, and a single quotation from him will be enough to complete the picture:

> Some wet and blowing weather having occasioned the port-holes to be shut, and the grating to be covered, fluxes and fevers among the negroes ensued. While they were in this situation, my profession requiring it, I frequently went down among them, till at length their apartments became so extremely hot as to be only sufferable for a very short time. But the excessive heat was not the only thing that rendered their situation intolerable. The deck, that is the floor of their rooms, was so covered with the blood and mucous which had proceeded from them in consequence of the flux, that it resembled a slaughter-house. It is not in the power of the human imagination to picture to itself a situation more dreadful or disgusting. Numbers of the slaves having fainted, they were carried up on deck, where several of them died, and the rest were with great difficulty, restored. It had nearly proved fatal to me also.   [quoted Pope-Hennessy, op. cit., p 102]

As for Captain Phillips and the *Hannibal*, in the end, out of his 700 negroes, he delivered only 372 alive in Barbados. They were sold for £19 a head.

The slaves were, of course, subject to the normal risks of seafaring – shipwreck, fire, tempest, and so on – and many of the craft in the trade never completed the second leg; but the biggest hazard from the owner's point of view, next to disease, was that propensity of the negroes for committing suicide. On occasions they did it in large groups simultaneously, as, for instance, in April 1737 when the *Prince of Orange*, having completed the passage, lay at St Christopher, with her captain, Japhet Bird, organising the sale of his cargo.

> At our arrival here [wrote one of those on board in a letter subsequently published in the *Boston Weekly News Letter*] I thought all our troubles of this voyage were over; but on the contrary I might say that dangers rest on the borders of security. On the 14th of March we found a great deal of discontent among the slaves, particularly the men, which

12 Manacles and leg irons used in the slave trade

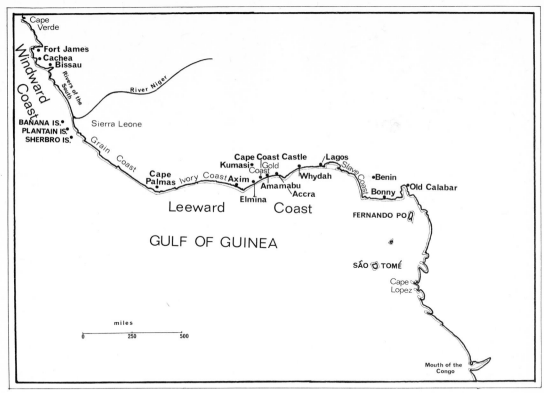

MAP NO. 5   The Guinea Coast, showing the principal slave ports

continued till the 16th about five o'clock in the evening when to our great amazement above an hundred men slaves jumped overboard . . . out of the whole we lost 33 of as good men slaves as we had on board, who would not endeavour to save themselves, but resolved to die and sunk directly down. Many more of them were taken up almost drowned, some of them died since, but not to the owner's loss, they being sold before any discovery was made of the injury salt water had done them.

[quoted Pope-Hennessy, op. cit., pp 105–6]

The slaves having been graded and sold like any other merchandise, the second leg of the triangle was complete; and the ship began preparations for the third and last one. The slave-shelves were taken down and the timber in them stowed as dunnage; then the fetters, branding-irons, and other tools of the trade were overhauled and carefully put away for future use. (These were, in fact, a very valuable part of the slave-ship's equipment and the ironmasters of the 18th century made and sold 'vast quantities of manacles, fetters, chains and padlocks, as well as branding-irons, for use when the ships were *slaved* . . .' and did very well out of the business.) Finally, the ship was thoroughly cleaned and as far as possible disinfected and cleared of the particularly repulsive kind of rat that haunted slave-ships. Then she was loaded with sugar and molasses consigned either to New England or Europe where it was sold to complete the triangle and provide capital for the next voyage.

It is interesting to note that the trade was a very big gamble and although huge fortunes were made in it, the profit was never certain and always unpredictable in size. Pope-Hennessy quotes the example of the snow *Africa*, a two-masted, square-rigged ship of 100 tons burthen which sailed from Bristol for New Calabar in the autumn of 1774. She was owned by a syndicate of eight Bristol merchants and was stocked up with 'the

31

usual trade goods – brandy, rum, guns, laced hats and waistcoats, Indian and Manchester cottons, multi-coloured china beads, iron bars, copper rods and so on'. Her cargo cost £4,445 14s. and when the ship had been fitted out ready for sea a total of £5,692 16s. had been invested in the voyage. Command was given to a Captain George Merrick, a man well versed in the Guinea Trade, and he had written instructions to proceed to New Calabar and exchange his cargo,

> for good healthy young negroes and ivory, and . . . not to buy any old slaves or children but good healthy young men and women, and buy all the ivory you can and when you are half-slaved don't stay too long if there is a possibility of getting off for the risk of sickness and mortality then become great. . . . [quoted Pope-Hennessy, op. cit., p. 109]

He was expressly warned about taking naked lights near the rum or the gunpowder and recommended to treat the negroes as well as circumstances would permit.

Captain Merrick disposed of his slaves at St Vincent and also got rid of almost half his crew of 31 hands, making the third leg of the triangle in ballast with a crew of 17, only 12 of whom had sailed with him to New Calabar. The negroes were sold for a total of £5,128 12s. 6d. and the ship showed a loss on the voyage.

It is argued that the *Africa* was an exceptional case and against her can be set the *Enterprize* of Liverpool, with a net profit of £25,000 for a single voyage on the triangle via Bonny and Havana. That was in 1803–4. Three years before that the *Louisa*, another Liverpool ship, got back from Jamaica with nearly £20,000. In 1805 the *Fortune*, also from Liverpool, made her second leg from the Congo to the Bahamas and showed a profit of over £13,000, which the owners appear to have considered as merely a slightly superior kind of chicken-feed. That particular profit was bought dearly and

> The *Fortune* scarcely lived up to its name, for the slaves sold slowly, and during the long delay, the trading mate and one sailor ran off, thirty-four of the seamen were impressed into, or volunteered for, the Royal Navy at Nassau, the third mate and six seamen died on the voyage, and two of the other sailors were drowned.   [ibid., p 110]

The centre of the Triangular Trade in England was undoubtedly Liverpool, and the people of the town grew fat on the proceeds of it. Towards the end of the 18th century – 1783 to 1793 – 'there were ten merchant houses of major importance' in the business and behind them were another 349 firms less well known. All of them did very well out of it and 'attorneys, drapers, ropemakers, grocers, tallow chandlers, barbers', citizens of every class and calling, fell over themselves to invest in the voyages. The fact is that the element of risk in the trade was never as great as it seemed, largely because the prime cost of negroes on the Coast varied little and was seldom boosted much even in times of short supply, while the price of their food on the passage was reckoned at a mere 10s. per head. Pope-Hennessy estimates the gain on each slave sold at 'well over thirty per cent' and declares that in the ten-year period mentioned above 'the net profit to the town of Liverpool on an aggregate of 303,737 slaves sold was almost three million pounds or about 300,000 pounds per annum . . .' (ibid., p 145).

The geography of the Guinea Coast is confusing because of the way the various stretches overlap, but for the seafarer it was divided first into the Windward and the Leeward Coasts, the former being the portion west of Cape Palmas and the latter that to the east of it, or putting it another way, the Windward Coast fronted the Atlantic and the Leeward Coast faced south into the Gulf of Guinea. The Windward Coast included Senegambia, Rivers of the South, Sierra Leone, and the Grain Coast. The

TO BE SOLD, on board the Ship *Bance-Iſland*, on tueſday the 6th of *May* next, at *Aſhley-Ferry* ; a choice cargo of about 250 fine healthy NEGROES, juſt arrived from the Windward & Rice Coaſt. —The utmoſt care has already been taken, and ſhall be continued, to keep them free from the leaſt danger of being infected with the SMALL-POX, no boat having been on board, and all other communication with people from *Charles-Town* prevented.

Auſtin, Laurens, & Appleby.

N. B. Full one Half of the above Negroes have had the SMALL-POX in their own Country.

principal slaving ports in it were Banana Island, Plantain Island, Sherbro, Bissau, and Gallinas River. The Leeward Coast included the Ivory Coast, the Gold Coast, the Slave Coast, and such famous ports as Elmina, Cape Coast Castle, Anamabu, Whydah, Bonny, and Old Calabar.

In some of these places – notably Elmina or the *Castle of the Mine* – relics of the Triangular Trade still exist, as they do on a smaller scale in the museums of seaports once involved in it; but when even these last traces of the traffic are gone, the scarifying memory of it will live on in the minds of men. It has gone too deep in the African peoples for them to forget. As Morton points out, the slave raids resulted in a 'never-ending series of tribal wars and the devastation of immense areas . . .' and, he adds,

> It is probably to these wars that the elements of brutality, fear and superstition in African culture, of which so much has been heard, are mainly attributable.   [op. cit., p 467n]

Altogether this is one chapter in his history about which the seafarer can feel only shame and remorse.

————————— 4 ▭————————

It would be quite wrong to imagine that the business of seafaring people as carriers was dominated in the 18th century by the three great trades described above. Important as they were, the Guinea Coast, East Indies, and West Indies at this time represented the growing-points, so to speak, and the great bulk of shipping was still concentrated elsewhere. In 1806, for example, when, as already noted, 652 ships cleared outward from British ports to the British West Indies and 63 to the East Indies, a total of 5,100 left for other destinations. The full list reads:

To: Denmark and Norway	1,374	Africa	170
Br. West Indies	652	East Indies	63
Germany	618	Italy	61
Russia	591	France	36
United States	538	Malta	25
Holland	455	West Indies (foreign)	15
British North America	343	Cape of Good Hope	14
Sweden	318	Danzig	14
Portugal and Madeira	311	New South Wales	2
Prussia	316		

[quoted J. Holland Rose, op. cit., p 238]

This 'commercial priority of Europe at that time over the other continents' is demonstrated further in Schlote's figures already quoted. These show that at the end of the 18th century, British exports to Europe were still slightly more than half of her outward trade (55·2 per cent) and her imports from the same area stood at one-third (32·7 per cent).

What then were these ships carrying during the years of expanding empire, while the Guineamen hauled their loads of suffering black flesh across the second leg of the infamous triangle, the East Indiamen hurried homeward with their silks and spices, and the West Indiamen with their sugar and tobacco? The answer is to be found in the records of the wool trade, the archives of almost forgotten chartered companies like the 15th-century *Merchant Adventurers*, the *Eastland Company*, and the *Turkey Company*, and, obliquely, in the diaries of Samuel Pepys.

Taking them as they come to mind, the Merchant Adventurers was formed for the express purpose of exporting cloth to northern Europe. This particular Company went out of existence in 1578, but the trade continued to flourish and J. Massie, writing in 1764, said:

> . . . the exports of woollen cloth, which under Charles II 'did not much exceed the yearly value of one million pounds, amounted in 1699 to almost three millions sterling, from which vast sum, with occasional ebbings and flowings, our annual exports of Woollen Manufactures have gradually risen to full four millions of late years.'

[quoted Morton, op. cit., p 326]

Some of that has been glimpsed on its way to China, but only a tiny portion of the whole, and the balance would add up to a pretty sizeable number of ship-loads for northern European ports. This would be a large part of the Eastland Company's outward trade with Scandinavian and Baltic countries, and their ships would load timber and tar homewards, squeezing in the odd consignment of Russian furs to make up the value. There are repeated references in Pepys to the Baltic timber trade. On 21 July 1664, for example, he made a contract with Sir W. Warren for 'almost 1000 Gothenburg masts, the biggest that ever were made in the Navy', and again on 18 October in the same year he 'made a very great contract with Sir W. Warren for £3,000 load of timber'. Timber was also shipped from the New England colonies and of course there was the codfish from the Grand Banks of Newfoundland, both trade routes outside the scope of the Indiamen and the triangle.

Then there was the Turkey Company and the eastern Mediterranean, where the competition with the French and the Venetians was fierce and often bloody, and the seafarer's neck was also in hazard from the Barbary pirates based along the North

African coast. The Turkey Company 'had the great advantage over the private trader that it could send out a powerful fleet each year, capable of resisting all attacks'. The Company was originally formed in 1581, but it was reconstituted in 1601, and from then till the later half of the 18th century it enjoyed a virtual monopoly of trade with Turkey, '. . . exporting cloth and importing silk, drugs and other Eastern produce' (Morton, op. cit., p 201).

The citrus fruit trade from the Western Isles – the Madeiras and the Azores – was another rather special line of business for the seaman and he had to be good at it. Small, fast schooners were employed on this route. They were built for speed and carried a lot of sail, and at one time between 200 and 300 of them were scurrying up and down the Western Approaches with their cargoes of oranges and lemons for the London market. Fruit in the shape of grapes and currants from such ports in the Levant as Smyrna and Patras occupied another sizeable fleet.

Everything in these ships, even carrying capacity itself, took second place to speed, and calms, not gales and high-running seas, were the bugbear of their masters. Joseph Conrad, writing in the last decades of the sailing-ship era about such a calm in the vicinity of the Western Isles, says:

> From the main truck of the average tall ship the horizon describes a circle of many miles, in which you can see another ship right down to her waterline; and these very eyes which follow this writing have counted in their time over a hundred sail becalmed, as if within a magic ring, not very far from the Azores – ships more or less tall. There were hardly two of them heading exactly the same way, as if each had meditated breaking out of the enchanted circle at a different point of the compass. But the spell of the calm is a strong magic. The following day still saw them scattered within sight of each other and heading different ways; but when, at last, the breeze came with the darkling ripple that ran very blue on a pale sea, they all went in the same direction together. For this

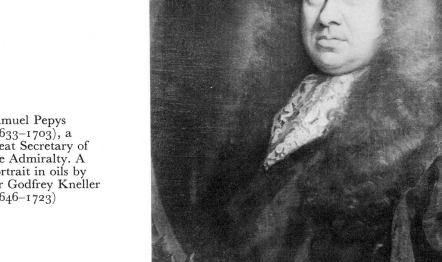

14 Samuel Pepys (1633–1703), a great Secretary of the Admiralty. A portrait in oils by Sir Godfrey Kneller (1646–1723)

35

was the homeward-bound fleet from the far-off ends of the earth, and a Falmouth fruit-schooner, the smallest of them all, was heading the flight. One could have imagined her very fair, if not divinely tall, leaving a scent of lemons and oranges in her wake.

[*The Mirror of the Sea*, pp 35–6]

There was also at this time – before a modern road system had been developed anywhere in Europe and when railways were still a dream – an enormous volume of coastwise shipping. It employed a wide assortment of craft – luggers, brigs, spritsail barges, ketches, schooners, snows, pinks, and so on – and they carried such unromantic cargoes as coal, lime, quarried stone for building, salt herring, and home-grown timber. Deep-water men have always been a little scornful of this type of seafaring. *Dog-barking navigation* was their name for it, the legend being that the masters of coasters groped a passage from a sheep-dog barking on one headland to a terrier yapping on the next. But this was the school in which James Cook learned the trade and when it came to seamanship he was and is still second to none.

Another seafaring trade flourishing in the 18th century was the Arctic whaling. Here the product was oil and whalebone and the seaman was hunter and producer as well as the carrier. In the early part of the century most of the Greenland whaling was done out of northern European continental ports, and England had little or no part in it. For example, in 1721 there were in the Arctic a total of 445 whale-ships and the number was made up of:

251 Hollanders	55 Hamburgers	20 Biscainers
90 Danes	24 out of Bremen	5 Norwegians

From these figures it is obvious that the Dutch and Germans dominated the trade at this time, and Lubbock records the following statistics in confirmation of the fact:

In the ten years between 1699 and 1708 the Dutch sent out 1652 whalers and killed 8537 whales, which sold for $4\frac{3}{4}$ million florins.

and between 1617 and 1719:

2289 ships sailed from Hamburg, of which 84 were wrecked, the 2205 ships brought home 444,607 casks of blubber, the produce of 9976 whales. . . .

[Lubbock, *The Arctic Whalers*, p 82]

The ill-starred South Sea Company (of Bubble fame) was first to attempt a revival of English whaling. This was in 1725 when the Company began operating with 12 ships especially built for the trade. No expense was spared in fitting out and manning them and only the best was good enough; they even brought over German masters to command their vessels, German harpooners to kill their whales, and German blubber-cutters to flense them, while for base they took over a whole dock at Rotherhithe and re-equipped it. The result was dismal failure. In eight seasons they spent over £250,000, lost 4 ships, built another 13, and after selling up showed a net loss on the venture of £177,782 3s. (ibid., p 83). Lubbock, after giving these details, adds:

Such a result at a time when it was reckoned that three whales per ship meant a profit, and one good year made up for six bad ones, explains the 'South Sea Bubble'. . . . [ibid.]

In 1733 a bounty of 20s. a ton was paid to encourage English ships and seamen to enter the trade, but though this was increased to 30s. a ton seven years later, it had little effect and it was not until 1750 when the bounty was raised to 40*s*. a ton that the English began to have any significant hand in what had become known as *the Greenland fishing*. Meanwhile, it continued to be dominated by the Dutch.

> In 1736 there were no less than 251 whalers from Holland, 55 from Hamburg, 55 from Bremen, 20 Biscainers and 5 from Bergen. . . . In 1739 there were 5 English whalers at Greenland, which took 11½ whales, as compared with 133 Dutch ships at Greenland which took 678 whales and 55 Dutch ships at Davis Straits, which took 51 whales. [ibid., p 85]

Ten years after that it was still the Dutch who, in addition to the vast body of experience accumulated down the years, seemed to have a special aptitude for the hunt and the processing. In 1749 they had 114 ships in the Spitzbergen area and 41 in the Davis Strait, the first fleet killing a total of 412 whales and the second another 206. From then on, however, ships out of English and Scottish ports, as well as New Englanders out of Nantucket, increased in numbers season by season while the size of the Dutch stake diminished. In 1770 50 English ships and 9 Scottish ships went north to the ice-rim and returned with a total of 2,238 tons of blubber. In the same season the Nantucket fleet numbered 125 ships and they brought home '14,331 barrels of oil, worth about 358,200 dollars'.

A first-hand account of a voyage made in 1772 by the Whitby whaler *Volunteer* is preserved in a book published by her surgeon who is otherwise unidentified, and among the many invaluable details to be culled from it are a number of hard facts about manning and pay. The *Volunteer* was an eight-boat ship and 'carried six men to each boat', together with six harpoons, six lances, and seven lines. So her total crew consisted 'of a captain, 2 mates, 2 carpenters, a "specsineerer" [chief harpooner and general top-hand], 7 harpooners [the master was also rated a harpooner, making eight

MAP NO. 6   Haunts of the Greenland Whale

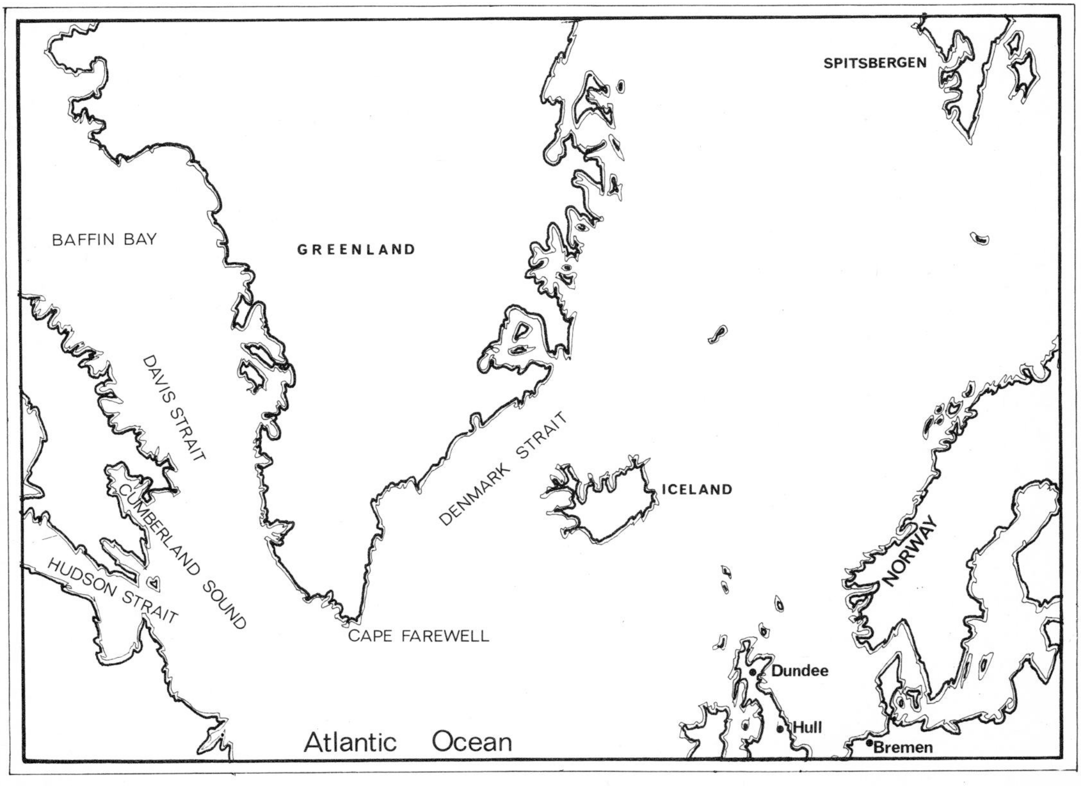

in all], 8 boat-steerers, 8 line managers, 8 apprentices, 2 cooks and 24 seamen' (quoted, ibid., p 113). On pay the same source gives the following details:

> The monthly pay of the crew was: Mate, carpenter and surgeon, £3 10s. each; second mate and carpenter's mate, £2 10s. each; boat-steerers, £2; line managers, £1 15s.; seamen and cooks £1 10s. each. The captain received a bounty of 21 guineas, speck-sineerer 9 guineas and the harpooners 8 guineas each. The captain and specsineerer also had six shillings for every ton of oil and the harpooners 5s. 3d. each. The reward to the harpooner who struck and killed a fish was half a guinea, besides which the captain received 3 guineas, the surgeon 21s., the mates, specsineerer and carpenter 10s. 6d. each, the carpenter's mate and boat-steerers 5s. each, line managers, seamen and cooks 2s. 6d. each for every fish killed.   [quoted ibid.]

This was good money for the time, but they earned it. Hunting the Greenland whale was indeed a man-size job and there was no room in the ships for layabouts or seekers of soft options. Whaling-men were hard, the toughest maybe ever to tread a deck; they had to be, for the history of the trade has a very broad streak of tragedy running through it – men swept overboard, drowned in broken boats, dead in a score of different ways, all heart-stopping in their violence; and ships overwhelmed, ships crushed in the ice, ships that sailed and were never heard of again.

The Greenland fishery reached its peak in 1788 when 255 ships sailed north in it from English and Scottish ports. Eight of them were lost in the ice.

But the Greenland whaling, the Baltic timber, the citrus fruit trade, and all the other European preoccupations of the carriers so far noted, although important, were in a sense blind shoots; they were nothing new and on them the seafarer was more or less marking time. What really mattered in this period was the activity of Abraham Darby of Coalbrookdale, who around 1760 began smelting iron with coal instead of charcoal. By 1765 his new process had superseded the old and 'the number and size of the blast furnaces increased yearly'. The production of pig-iron 'which was only 17,350 tons in 1740 had risen to 68,300 tons in 1788 and to 125,079 tons in 1796'. So too with coal, the amount mined annually increasing fourfold – from 2,600,000 tons to over 10 million tons – between 1700 and 1795. This all added up to more cargoes for the

15   The Hull whalers *Friends* and *Molly*, by F. Fletcher (1787)

carriers both out and home, and by the end of the century they were running high-grade iron ore in bulk over the North Sea from Sweden and out of Spanish ports northwards across the Bay of Biscay.

The *Industrial Revolution,* as it is called, was under way.

━━━◁ 5 ▷━━━

Four of the greatest names in the history of seafaring belong to: (*a*) a 17th-century shipwright; (*b*) one of the craft he designed and constructed; (*c*) a yard in London where ships were built; and (*d*) a man who owned them.

The first, Phineas Pett, goes a long way back. In 1612 he became Master of the Shipwrights' Hall and by that time he had already taken a M.A. degree and learned about ships the hard way – by sailing in them. Thus his theoretical education was matched by his practical experience and, backed by a remarkable freedom from the inhibiting effects of traditionalism in his thinking, he introduced an amazing number of improvements into shipbuilding. Altogether his influence was wide and it lasted far beyond his own time. The most famous of the ships he built was the *Sovereign of the Seas.* She was the first three-decker and so big – as well as so costly by the standards of her time – that his plans for her met extremely heavy opposition. But Phineas thrived on that and his dream-ship was completed in spite of it. She was 1,640 tons burthen, 128 feet long in the keel, 168 feet on the waterline, 232 feet overall, with a maximum beam of 48 feet, and she cost £300,000 to build – which was not far short of a king's ransom in those days. Her three decks were flush and on top of them she had a fore-castle, a half-deck, a quarter-deck, and a round-house. Present-day experts reckon her old-fashioned beak-head bow was too high for seaworthiness; but not much record of her achievements survives. Nevertheless, she was about for a long time, in the end being destroyed by fire in the Medway in 1696.

It was with the *Prince Royal,* however, that Phineas Pett made his great contribution to the development of the sailing ship, and this is the second great name in the business. She has been described as 'the parent of all future men-of-war' and her design conditioned the thinking of naval architects right down into the 19th century. Frank C. Bowen, in his book *From Carrack to Clipper,* says:

> She was a remarkably fine-looking ship, the old beak-bow of the galley days being very considerably modified and improved, the freeboard being comparatively low, the decks flush and the wales having but little sheer. The bow and stern lines were a joy to the lover of ships and would not disgrace a naval architect of any age. [p 22]

By this time the round stern was beginning to take the place of the square tuck; but the wood-carver still had an exaggerated importance and this had the effect of inhibiting change. Another drag was the corruption in government services which could only be checked by making rules and regulations so stringent and rigid that they were akin to Holy Writ, and nobody dared to step outside them. It is worth noting in this connection that France, Spain, Sweden, and Denmark in this period all possessed finer and bigger ships than England, and it was not until the latter part of the 18th century that British naval craft became supreme.

With the Indiamen of the Honourable John Company it was different. As an organisation it set a standard of excellence in everything it did right from the beginning, and this was maintained until the end. Nothing cheap, nothing shoddy, nothing mean;

39

no cheeseparing or pinching and scraping, and always only the best was good enough for both their ships and the men who ran them. In the early days most of the ships they 'took up' were built in the Blackwall Yard, the third of the names to conjure with. The first Blackwall East Indiaman was the *Globe*, which made a voyage to India in 1611 that lasted for five years and showed a profit of 218 per cent; the last were the two launched in 1825 – the *Abercrombie Robinson* (1,325 tons) and the *Edinburgh* (1,325 tons) – and that, although it was by no means the end of the Blackwall Yard's contribution to seafaring, adds up to 215 years of association.

Pepys was familiar with the yard and records visiting it on 15 January 1661:

> . . . we walked to the waterside, and in our way walked into the rope-yard, where I do look into the tar-houses and other places, and took great notice of all the several works belonging to the making of a cable. So after a cup of burnt wine at the tavern there, we took barge and went to Blackwall, and viewed the dock, and the new Wet Dock, which is newly made there, and a brave new merchantman which is to be launched shortly, and they say to be called the Royal Oak. . . . [pp 129–30]

In spite of its high principles and independence of spirit, however, the East India Company did not escape entirely from the side-effects of the 18th-century *malaise*. Some of them were unavoidable, whatever the will; and Lubbock notes that East Indiamen varied very little in size during the century. Towards the end of it they were still seldom over 700 tons, and he puts this down to the way the Admiralty hogged the supply of timber for knees and frames. One of the regulations referred to above reserved every oak knee and elbow over a certain size for the Navy, and this restricted the possible size of merchant ships until someone dreamed up iron knees and brackets. Other improvements introduced first in East Indiamen were the round-headed rudder and a capstan with iron instead of hardwood parts. In the end the superiority of the Indiamen was so marked that even the Admiralty woke up to it and asked the East India Company's surveyor for suggestions that might improve the efficiency and durability as well as the seaworthiness of naval vessels. The surveyor – his name was Gabriel Snodgrass – obliged and he pulled no punches: '. . . all men-of-war were too short and stepped their masts too far forward', he declared; then he put the naval pundits wise about how to season and preserve timber, advised that ships should be built under cover, and commented caustically on the folly of saving money by making the bottoms and the sheathing too thin. (Copper sheathing as a protection against the teredo worm had come in with the *Alarm*, a frigate built in 1761.)

The fourth great name of the period is that of Robert Wigram, son of a Bristol shipmaster and born in Wexford of an Irish mother in 1743. He never knew his father, who was lost at sea, but he was well brought up by an uncle and his mother, and at the age of 19 went up to London to study medicine. In two years he had qualified and shipped as surgeon on board the East Indiaman, *Admiral Watson* (400 tons). The voyage lasted two years and nine months and in the course of it, Wigram established a close friendship with her second mate, William Money, that was to last the whole of his life. Altogether Wigram was at sea for eight years, during which time he made three voyages, and finally contracted a disease of the eyes which forced him to give up his work as a surgeon. His next venture was into the drug trade, then in 1788 he invested his savings in the purchase of his first East Indiaman. She was the *General Goddard* (755 tons) and he bought her from his old friend and former shipmate, William Money. The ship was immediately taken up, i.e. chartered, by the East India Company and did very well for Wigram; but his real money-spinner was a ship he had built for himself in 1790 at Wells' Yard, Deptford. She was the *True Briton* (1,198 tons), the first of the name, and a perfect illustration of the advances the three-masted ship had made up to that date.

Starting with her hull, the first thing noticed about her was how little change there had occurred at the ends of it; the old beak-bow – modified to some extent perhaps, but still recognisable and almost as old-fashioned as seafaring itself – and the flat stern with its square counter were still there, but the towering forecastle and piled-up poop had gone. She sat comparatively low in the water and, though there was still sheer, it was so perfectly balanced with the rest of her that she looked almost straight. The size of her was, of course, another significant and important development.

So too with her rig. Again it was the persistent features that caught the eye – the simple sail plan, limited to courses, lower and upper topsails, and as yet no topgallant

17   The East Indiaman *True Briton* (1790), 1,198 tons, drawn and
      engraved by C. Turner

sails or royals; the massive, steeply tilted bowsprit and the spritsail still there underneath it – but the jibboom was new and the jib as well as the forestaysail. It was the mizzen, however, that had changed most. The old lateen sail that used to be carried there had been altered out of all recognition. The part of it forward of the mast was gone completely, the great canted yard had become a gaff, the sail itself had a boom, and the mast both lower and upper topsails.

The *True Briton* was a very successful Indiaman and there was about her more than a hint of the beauty of the ultimate sailing ship. She made eight voyages for John Company, the last in the 1808–9 season when she was lost without a trace in the China Sea.

Robert Wigram went on building ships and before long had acquired a controlling interest in the Blackwall Yard. He was a most successful India husband and in the 25 years over the turn of the century owned a total of 21 ships which made 139 voyages under the East India Company's gridiron flag. He was also interested in rope-making, breweries, and politics, yet found time to become Chairman of the East India Docks and to father 17 sons.

Ships built for one trade quite often finished up in another one quite different, but, broadly speaking, the first consideration of the designer was the purpose for which he was building and this made for an extraordinary variety of vessels being in use at any given time. Thus, the north-east coast collier brigs had special qualities of strength, stability, and handiness which made Captain Cook choose two of them – the *Endeavour* and the *Discovery* – for his exacting voyages into the South Seas. Lubbock mentions another – the *Brotherly Love* (214 tons) of South Shields, which was built at Ipswich in 1764 and was sunk in collision off the Yorkshire coast over a hundred years later. She was 86·5 feet long, 24 feet beam, and 17 feet deep, and her working life was 115 years, which for a wooden ship must take some beating.

The Arctic whalers are another case in point. Newspaper advertisements around the end of the century give a hint of their size and shape. For instance:

London, November 21, 1787

For Sale by Candle

Over on N.W. part of the Royal Exchange, London,
on Friday the 30th instant, at one o'clock

The Good Ship *GREENLAND*,
with all her fishing stores.

Square stern, head and quarter galleries, British build, burthen 290 tons. Well calculated in the Greenland Fishery and completely fitted for the purpose, having been docked and in complete repair and may be sent to sea without any expense except provisions.

Her boats, lines, etc., nearly new, having been but once used.

For particulars inquire of John Garford and Co., Brokers, Clements Lane, Lombard Street.

[quoted Lubbock, *The Arctic Whalers*, p 125]

18 Whaler *Munificence* of Hull, by R. Willoughby (*c.* 1802)

Another from the same source reads:

To be Sold by Private Contract

The good ship *Advice*, square stern, Whitby built, 207 tons measurement, will carry 17 keels of coals, is calculated for the Baltic, Greenland, coal or coasting trade on a light draught of water, takes the ground well, shifts without ballast, sails remarkably fast, well found with all kinds of stores and may be sent to sea at an easy expense; had a thorough repair last winter at Whitby, and now lying at Hull Dock.

For further particulars apply to
Captain Thomas Garbutt at Sunderland, near Whitby, or Mr. Nathan Wood, in Hull.

[ibid., p 149]

The illustration above shows three Greenland whalers about their business. The ice-rim on the left with the floes among the ships demonstrate vividly the hazards these men faced. But the real interest is in the ships. Here the square stern and the quarter galleries mentioned in the advertisement above are instantly recognisable; and the hull of the *Munificence* is seen to be quite a different shape to that of the Indiaman. There is the same enormous bowsprit and soaring jibboom, but she is floating higher and the echo of the piled-up stern of the century before is inescapable. There is not much difference in the rig, however, and both vessels shown under sail have the spanker with a gaff on the mizzen instead of the older lateen sail.

So in spite of the incessant wars of the 18th century, ships continued to grow in size and advance in sophistication; but the naval architect was still lumbered with the two age-old and apparently inescapable problems of the seafarer – hogging and stability. In

43

other words, whether his brief was to design an Indiaman or a collier brig, a Guinea Coast slaver or a Greenland whaler, his length was limited by the need to preserve longitudinal strength and his capacity by the demands of stability; and notwithstanding all the progress that had been made, the real breakthrough was still to come.

6

Of all the wars referred to above, two had special significance for seafarers and enormously far-reaching effects on their way of life. They were the American War of Independence (1774–83) and the Napoleonic Wars (1793–1815).

Given the whole history of the British colonies and an awareness of the irresistible drive to expand which possessed the peoples of the world, including colonists, in those days, the conflict which resulted in the American Declaration of Independence seems to have been inevitable and the politicians particularly blind not to have seen it coming. The ostensible issue was the right of the English Parliament to tax the colonies, but the trouble went deeper. Right at the bottom of it were the Navigation Acts and the determination of the old country to prevent industrial development in the new; and the incident that sparked it all off was the famous *Boston Tea Party*. As already noted, the imports of tea by the East India Company had increased at this time to over 10½ million lbs. per annum and it was becoming a considerable headache to everybody concerned.

> In 1773 the English Company was terribly overstocked with tea, and was on the verge of bankruptcy; and, to relieve it, the ministers of George III obtained the authority of Parliament to give a drawback for the entire amount of the English duty; but, in order to assert their right to tax, they imposed a very moderate duty of 3*d*. a lb. to be collected at the port of discharge in the colonies. The result was the Boston Tea Party of December 16, 1773. [Morse, op. cit., vol II, p 296]

Green describes the affair as

> a trivial riot . . . the arrival of some English ships laden with tea kindled fresh irritation in Boston, where the non-importation agreement was strictly enforced. A mob in the disguise of Indians boarded the vessels and flung their contents into the sea. . . .
> [*A Short History of the English People*, p 753]

The London Parliament retorted by closing the port against all commerce, altering the Colony's charter, and withdrawing 'the liberties it had enjoyed ever since the Pilgrim Fathers landed on its soil'. Men who had crossed the Atlantic and hacked a new life out of virgin land in the name of freedom could not be expected to stand for this kind of pushing around; they took to arms on Bunkers Hill.

The immediate effect of the American war on the seafarer was the disruption of his normal occupation on the well-established trade routes. Traffic still shuttled along on the triangle, Indiamen still battled home round the Cape with their loads of tea and silk, and the whalers out of Hull and Whitby continued to hunt off Greenland and up into the Davis Strait; but the war did not help and life went on under new pressures and subject to additional hazards.

The fighting was a long way off and, whatever consolation there was in this for the people sitting snug at home waiting for the arrogant colonists to be brought to heel, it was no comfort to the sailorman. At first it was thought four regiments would be enough

44

for the task, but reinforcements were soon urgently required. Ships were needed to carry them across the Atlantic and more ships to supply them once they had got there, and it began to seem there would be no end to it. As the build-up continued, more and more shipping capacity was absorbed and all kinds of vessels from colliers and whalers to stately Indiamen were taken up by the government for transports. It is to be assumed that as always in such circumstances the owners made money; but for the seamen it was different. Again, as always, they contributed the blood and sweat, and suddenly they were in great demand and very short supply.

And now as he went about his lawful business the seafarer was faced with two risks which, in his own phrase, 'he never signed for'. They were the *press* and the *privateers*. Neither of them was new.

The press was a method of recruiting foremast hands for the Royal Navy and in spite of its complete denial of the elementary human rights – particularly a man's free will – it was entirely legal. A naval commander needing seamen to make up his crew obtained a warrant 'for the impressment of men', then sent out his press-gang. This usually consisted of a captain and two lieutenants and a group of ratings especially selected for their toughness and ability to come out of a rough-house on top. Any able-bodied man, seaman or landlubber, was liable to be pressed and in hard times the press-gangs were not above making sorties inland, whereby many a farmer's boy who didn't know a bowline from a bowsprit found himself whisked off to sea with a broken head to nurse if he protested; but naturally tarpaulins were preferred, so the gangs usually operated after dark and their happiest hunting-grounds were the waterfront dives of seaports.

The press bore particularly savagely on the Greenland whalers. Those who sailed in that trade were a special breed, truly *seldom* men, and a couple of them would be considered worth half a dozen run of the mill deckhands and twice that number of clodhoppers. Lubbock records that by the end of 1778 'seamen were very scarce, especially in the northern ports', and he quotes cases such as the *Humber* which went up into the Davis Strait that year with 11 first-trippers in its crew of 40 and the *Leeds Industry* with 9 out of 42 and 6 of the others mere apprentices.

19   The Boston Tea
      Party (1773)

45

Privateering was another form of legalised crime practised against the sailorman. The privateers were:

> . . . armed vessels owned and officered by private individuals, but acting under a commission from the State, known as *letters of marque*, which allowed the owners to keep the prizes they captured, and granted them £5 for every man of the enemy killed or taken.
>
> [*Everyman's Encyclopedia*, vol 10, p 238]

Besides being authorised by the commission the practice was sanctified by the length of time it had been in existence and justified by its universality. Everybody – French, Dutch, Americans, and what have you – did it and somehow that made it all right for the British, though nobody has ever explained why. William Dampier did a bit of privateering in his day and Robert Wigram's *General Goddard* had a stab at it in 1795 against the Dutch while homeward bound on a voyage for John Company. She was one of a pack hunting out of St Helena and shared in prize-money totalling £76,664 14*s*. The record does not say how many of the £5 bonuses were included in this sum nor how many Dutch seamen died in the making of it. Lubbock produces some almost incredible figures on privateering in the American war.

> Between the autumn of 1778 and the spring of 1779, 120 privateers of 30,787 tons, carrying 1986 guns and 8754 men, were fitted out at Liverpool. . . .,
>
> [*The Arctic Whalers*, p 117]

and the Americans were in on it too. Their most famous privateer was the *General Mifflin*, a brig armed with 20 six-pounder guns, 20 swivels, and 170 men. The havoc she wrought in two weeks that summer included:

MAP NO. 7   Important names in the Napoleonic Wars. Villeneuve, the French commander, tried to tie Nelson in the West Indies, while he sped back to relieve the blockaded French fleet at Brest and get into the English Channel. He was intercepted and had to make for Cadiz, dreams of an invasion of England dispelled. The chase was a prelude to Trafalgar, where English supremacy at sea was confirmed

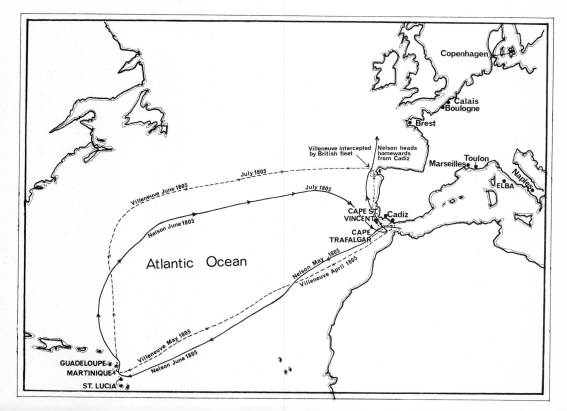

Chatham, with deals from Norway, plundered and set on fire.

Lion, from Leith to Archangel, stripped and scuttled.

Archangel Packet, from Archangel to London with 1000 barrels of tar and 1600 masts, which Captain McNeil sent to France, taking all but two of her crew aboard the privateer.

Dispatch, of London for Onega, plundered, left some of her people on board and kept her in company as a tender.

Dick, of Liverpool, 750 barrels of tar, 1000 masts, oars, etc., sent to France.

Sally, from Hull to Archangel, made into a store ship, putting all anchors, cables and sails plundered from other ships aboard her.

George, of Yarmouth, plundered, masts cut away and scuttled.   [ibid.]

In Drake's day the Spaniards tried to protect their merchant ships from privateers (or pirates, as they were more honestly called) by sailing a number of vessels in company so that between them they might muster greater fire-power and more men than any potential attacker. This was the beginning of convoys and the system was being extensively used by both sides before the American war was over. Later, in the Napoleonic Wars, special escort vessels were provided to do the fighting if necessary; but this meant more men being pressed and the ordinary seafarer, wanting only to get on with his job, must have cursed the recurrent wars and the politicians who made them happen.

Nevertheless, in the long term the effect of the American war on seafaring was beneficial. Contrary to all expectations the loss of the colonies resulted in an enormous increase in trade. Condliffe says:

> . . . British trade with the United States revived strongly after their achievement of independence. . . . Cotton was pouring in from the United States to feed the hungry looms of Lancashire. The tobacco trade was more flourishing than ever. Wheat was beginning to come to Britain from New York and New England. There was more trade and shipping between Britain and the independent United States than there ever had been with the dependent colonies. . . .   [op. cit., p 253]

And Green from a different angle and in a very different day and age noted that 'the war added a hundred million pounds to the National Debt but the burden was hardly felt. The loss of America only increased the commerce with that country' (op. cit., p 768). So much for colonialism and such sacred cows as the Navigation Acts!

The increased overseas trade of the newly independent United States of America is reflected in the number of American ships at Canton. In the season of 1790 there were only 6; in 1800 there were 23 and in 1804 36 out of a grand total of 79, only 39 of which were English. Morse records:

> The 36 American ships had a total of 10,720 tons burthen, an average of 297 tons; included therein were 7 brigs of or under 200 tons, and 3 ships of or over 500 tons; 18 are noted as coming with furs or skins. . . .   [op. cit., vol II, p 417]

Between them the American ships brought in $2,207,400 in specie, which represents a lot of trade, but the real interest for the seafarer lies in the ships themselves – the number and size. Here already can be seen an expansion in the American shipbuilding industry that before long was to present a serious challenge to British supremacy in the field.

The other seafarer's war, i.e. that with Napoleon, was bloodier and wider spread than any conflict since Rome and Carthage were at each other's throats in ancient times.

With a short interval after the Treaty of Amiens in 1802 it lasted continuously from 1793 till the fall of Paris in April 1814 and even then the *hundred days* and Waterloo were still to come.

Napoleon was different things to different people. European peasant, professional soldier, career politician, English manufacturer, shipmaster, foremast hand – what you thought of him depended on who or what you were and where you stood in relation to the killing. For some he was a liberator, a new Messiah; for others he was the incarnation of evil and threatened the very foundations of their way of life; for others again he was a genius and his battles masterpieces; and for a few he was the easy way to money and power. When the slaughter was over, however, and the dust had settled the conflict was seen to have been the final round in the struggle for empire and Britain had won it.

J. Holland Rose describes the Napoleonic War, particularly after the Treaty of Amiens, as a struggle between *Land-power* and *Sea-power*. At times it looked a very close-run thing. In 1802, for example, Napoleon was so much on top that he was able to demand and get the return of all the territories taken by Britain since 1793. These included St Lucia, Guadeloupe, the Cape of Good Hope, and Pondicherry. He also barred British produce from all the lands under his control 'which entailed on us a trade loss of over £10,000,000 a year'. By the time the war broke out again in 1803 '. . . British trade was shut out from nearly all coasts from Hamburg to Venice, except those of Portugal . . .' (op. cit., p 224). But British trade – thanks mainly to British naval power – continued to grow. Taking the Port of London, for example, the average yearly numbers of ships clearing outwards increased from 11,673 in 1803 to 15,211 in 1811. Over the same period the strength of the British Navy was:

	Battleships in Commission	Frigates in Commission	Losses
1803	32	73	13
1811	107	137	20

and the total number of merchantmen under the British flag was:

	Sailing out of Br. Isles	Sailing out of the colonies
In 1803	17,516	3,361
In 1811	19,725	3,450

As to the havoc wrought on this enormous volume of shipping by the French, the figure for 1803 is missing, but for 1811 it was 470 ships and the effectiveness of the convoy system is shown by the fact that 'the rates of insurance at Lloyds for British Merchantmen declined from 8 per cent in 1806 to 5·3 per cent in 1812' (ibid., p 231).

Contemporary sources give an occasional glimpse of these convoys. Rose quotes one from the *Life of Lord de Saumarez* by Sir J. Ross.

> Some 1000 British merchantmen were anchored off the hostile Danish coast in mid-October 1810; they were guarded by H.M.S. *Victory* (her last commission), bearing the flag of Admiral Lord Saumarez, along with six battleships and six frigates. . . .
>
> [ibid., p 232]

And Lubbock gives two more from the *Naval Chronicle*:

> *Plymouth Report*, 10th December, 1800:– Passed by to the westward the immense large fleets for Oporto, the Straits, Lisbon and the West Indies, nearly 550 sail under convoy of

20 October 1806. Napoleon's triumphant entry into Berlin after defeating the Prussians at Jena.

the *Sea Horse*, of 36 guns; *Maidstone*, 32; *Alliance*, 44; *Chichester*, 44; *Serapis*, 44; *La Pique*, 44; *Harpy*, 18; and *Dromedary*, 24; a dead calm took them aback off the Eddystone and the whole horizon was covered with the floating commerce of Albion's proud Isles. The fog cleared off about noon, and presented with the setting sun, a spectacle from the high points of land round this port, at once grand, picturesque and interesting to every lover of his country's commerce and welfare.

and again:

Plymouth Report, 10th August, 1801:– This day presented a most beautiful scene from the Hoe, 200 sail laying to, becalmed from horizon to horizon, of East and West Indiamen, under convoy of the *Theseus*, 74 guns; *Santa Margarita*, 36 guns; and two other frigates. By 10 a.m. a fine breeze from E.N.E. sprang up, and the whole fleet by noon was clear of the Dodman Point.   [*The Blackwall Frigates*, p 7]

Gaudin, one of Napoleon's own finance Ministers, summed it all up in his memoirs. England's final success was due, he said, to her 'mastery of the seas, which assured to her the profits of the world's commerce, and thereby the means to gain powerful helpers whose interests were common with hers . . .' Mollien, another in the same line, was even more blunt than that. He said that England 'waged a warfare of modern times' and Napoleon 'one of ancient times', and Rose goes along with that verdict. Napoleon's thinking was in his view essentially Mediterranean:

. . . For in maritime affairs he was, and he remained, a scion of that landlocked sea. But by 1812, the longings of the European peoples turned towards the West and East Indies, whence came the cane sugar and coffee, the fine cotton and silk, which England alone now supplied . . . the needs of civilised man had become oceanic and world-wide.
                                                                    [op. cit., p 239]

That was the challenge of the times for the seafarer and, as shall be seen, he responded to it triumphantly and then paid the inevitable price of success.

The Stately Phase

Navigation and naval power are the children, not the parents – the
effect, not the cause – of commerce.

[J. R. McCulloch]

ALTHOUGH THE 18TH-CENTURY STRUGGLE for empire brought about great changes in seafaring, not only in terms of volume and kind, but also in size and design of ships, methods of running them, and the organisation behind shipping in general, there had been as yet no revolutionary break. The world, for all the discoverers and colonists had done to open it up, was still relatively unknown with Western mankind spread very thinly about it. As Condliffe puts it in *The Commerce of Nations*:

> A considerable effort of imagination is now required to recreate the picture of the trading world at the close of the Napoleonic wars – a sprinkling of settlement on the Atlantic seaboard of the United States, small penal settlements at Sydney and Hobart, no white settlement in New Zealand, a handful of Dutch at the Cape and of French in Canada, Japan a hermit kingdom, and China almost as unknown, India governed uneasily from the scattered coastal forts of the East India Company, Spanish America in its undeveloped colonial status, and Africa still the Dark Continent. In Europe the British were a nation of thirteen million. There was no Germany and no Italy. The Ottoman Empire was still intact. Austria-Hungary and Russia were the greatest continental powers, and Prussia had not yet begun to organize the German Reich.   [pp 208–9]

MAP NO. 8   The chief European overseas settlements in 1800

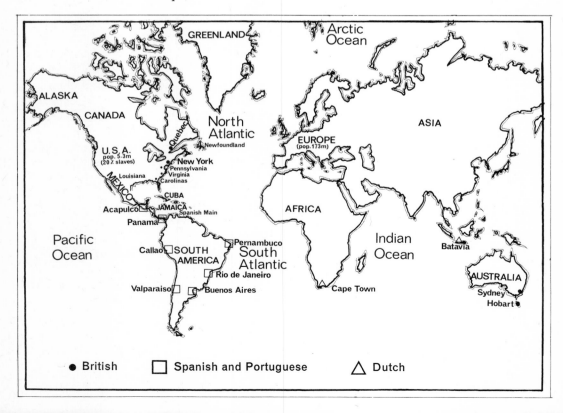

So empire had been won, but it still lacked two essentials – capital investment and people with skilled hands and/or organising brains to exploit it. But for the carriers, the objective conditions for the breakthrough already had been or were in course of being created.

———————◁ I ▷———————

Though ships are always at their best after the pilot is dropped and they are out and away, to function at all they need the land and land-based people, not only to produce and consume their cargoes, but to provide such facilities as harbours, warehouses, repair yards, and the men to run them. They also need merchants to back their voyages and financial wizards to stake them. In the early days all these things were provided on what might be called a *hand to mouth* basis, popping up here and there as and when required, and the business behind shipping was generally done in public places like taverns. The most famous of all these was Lloyd's Coffee-House.

The earliest surviving printed reference to Lloyd's appears in the *London Gazette* for 18–21 February 1689. It was then in Tower Street and two years later the owner, Mr Edward Lloyd, moved it to Lombard Street, where the premises quickly became famous as an auction-mart for ships and prize-goods, the resort of merchants, ship-owners, and shipmasters, and a place for the organisation of insurance policies on ships and cargoes.

Marine insurance had been developed by the Italian city states in the Middle Ages and was firmly established in England by the 16th century. In the beginning it was not a specialised business and the *underwriters*, as they were (and still are) called, could be pretty well anybody of substance. Wright and Fayle, for example, quote a John Gresham, 'who wrote £25 on the *Eli* in 1559', and he was a mercer and merchant adventurer. In 1601, however, an attempt was made to regularise underwriting and a Court of Assurances was set up by Act of Parliament. The preamble to the Act is worth quoting as a summary of the benefits of insurance:

> Whereas it hathe bene tyme out of mynde an usage amongste Merchantes, both of this Realme and of forraine Nacyons, when they make any greate adventure (speciallie into remote partes) to give some consideracon of Money to other psons (which commonlie are in noe small number) to have from them assurance made of their Goodes Merchandizes Ships and Things adventured . . . whiche course of dealinge is commonly termed a Policie of Assurance; by meanes of whiche Policies of Assurance it comethe to passe, upon the losse or perishings of any Shippe there followethe not the undoinge of any Man, but the losse lightethe rather easilie upon many, than heavilie upon fewe. . . .
>
> [Wright and Fayle, *History of Lloyds*, p 38]

The next significant legislation in marine insurance was an Act of 1720 which gave a monopoly in the business to two corporations, the Royal Exchange Assurance Corporation and the London Assurance Corporation. But by specifically prohibiting the insurance of ships and goods at sea by any other *corporation* or *partnership firm*, it left individuals free to underwrite on their own account, and in the end it was these private insurers, frequenting Lloyd's Coffee-House as a base, who came to dominate the whole world of marine insurance. The two corporations concentrated on fire and life insurance and 'at no time, probably, did they do more than about ten per cent. of the marine insurance carried on in London' (ibid., p 67).

After the death of Edward Lloyd, the Coffee-House passed by a marriage or two and other deaths into the hands of a Mr Thomas Jemson, who was a member of the Shipwrights' Company. To him goes the credit for establishing *Lloyd's List*, although he too was dead before the first issue came out in 1734. The List, published originally once a week, was brought out to satisfy 'the demand of the underwriters for shipping intelligence'. The earliest issue that has survived is the one for Friday, 2 January 1740, which is numbered No. 560 and carries the following notice:

> This List, which was formerly publish'd once a Week will now continue to be publish'd every *Tuesday* and *Friday*, with the Addition of the Stocks, Course of Exchange, &c – Subscriptions are taken in at Three Shillings per Quarter, at the Bar of *Lloyd's* Coffee-House in *Lombard Street*. Such Gentlemen as are willing to encourage this Undertaking, shall have them carefully deliver'd according to their Directions.   [quoted ibid., p 72]

At first the List was compiled from information supplied by individual frequenters of the house; but 'to the underwriter, even more than to the merchant and shipowner, prompt intelligence of arrivals, departures and casualties was of vital importance . . .' and a more comprehensive system had to be devised. This led to the appointment of correspondents in the principal seaports who sent in regular lists of arrivals and sailings; and by 1792, Lloyd's had 32 correspondents covering 28 ports.

In the early days the List was a single sheet, 12 inches by $7\frac{1}{2}$, with miscellaneous information on the front and shipping intelligence on the back. Among the commercial information given were current exchange rates 'at London on Dublin and fourteen continental centres', prices of gold and silver, and some Stock Exchange quotations. In the Marine List

21   The Subscribers' Room at Lloyds. A caricature by an
     unknown artist published in 1798

22 The earliest
surviving issue
of *Lloyd's List*

Gravesend ——— Arrived from		Eagle, Stavely	Biddiford
30 Dec. Draper, Leach	Dublin	Mary & Ellen, Rush	Leverpool
Katherine, Roberts	Figuera	——, Slade	ditto
Globe, Harvey	Lisbon	Fidelia. Monkheuse	Dublin
Expedition, Major	Gibralter	Mary-Ann, Craigh	Limerick
1 Industry, Sheppardson	Virginia	——, Neman	Gottenburg
Leostoff ——— arrived from		Nancy, Tracy	Madeira
Harwich ——— arrived from		Downs ——— Arrived from	
Success, Hartley	Gottenburg	30 K. of Portugal, Hughes	Lisbon
Leverpool ——— arrived from		Algarve, Olding	Faro
Deve, Drinkwater	Virginia	St. John, Farrel	Antigua
Leopard, —— ——	ditto	31 Webster, Stevens	Chester
Bristol ——— arrived from		Halsey & Suttle, Salisbury	ditto
31 Elizabeth, Cheshire	Antigua	1 Marys Reign, Jervoise	Barbadoes
Penzance ——— Arrived from		Wm. & Ann, Main	St. Kitts
Anne Sloop, Mitchel	Maderia	Brittania, Farmer	New-York
Falmouth ——— Arrived from			Remain for
27 Cleve, Rice	London	Two Dutch Ships	EastIndia
	Sailed for	A Dutch Ship	Guiney
Mary Galley, Cross	Gibralter	London, Pipon	Gibralter
Dartmouth ——— Arrived from		Concord, Spilman	Carolina
28 Greenwich, ——	London	Ann, Watson	Maryland
Faulker, —— ——	N.foundland	Swallow, Hutchinson	Philadelphia
30 Port Merch. Walls	Lisbon	Praleda, Herbert	Cork
	Came in for	Minabilla, Blake	Lisbon
Mercurius. Waddle	Lisbon	Ann, Ebsworthy	Guiney
Pool ——— Arrived from		Olliver, Pain	Gibralter
27 Watsons Adv. Watson	Lisbon	Nassau, Spilman	Falmouth
Rainbow, Skolds	ditto	Hannah, Kilpatrick	Portsmouth
Patience, Bowles	ditto	Paradox, Righton	St. Kitts
29 Betsy, Addis	Carolina		
31 Agnes & Mary, Pottle	N.foundland	*Winds at Deal.*	
Wm. & Thomas, Lander	London		
Cowes ——— Arrived from		30 SW 31 W 1 NW	
29 Brunswick, Payne	Carolina		
Carter, Cork	Alderney	Dublin ——— arrived from	
Nicholas, Hains	Cherburgh	Providence, Steward	London
		Edw. & Mary, Littler	ditto
	Came in for	Eagle,	ditto
St. Nicholas, Vesseur	Callais	Cork ——— Arrived from	
Concordia, Trock	Hamburg	15 Martha, Purkess	Southton
Hellena, Guillaume	Carolina	Jane & Betty, Jackson	Carolina
Dispatch, Wallace	Dublin	William, Higat	Isle of Man
Two Maries, Gordon	Southton	Margaret, Robinson	Dublin

. . . appear notices of the arrival of ships at Gravesend, 'Loestoff,' Harwich, 'Leverpool,' Bristol, Penzance, Falmouth, Dartmouth, 'Pool', Cowes, Southampton, Portsmouth, Dover, the Downs, Dublin and Cork. The information given, in each instance, comprises the date, ship's and Master's names, and port from whence arrived. In a few instances only, the list of arrivals is varied by notices of sailings, or the destination of ships touching at a port of call. The direction of the wind at Deal on the last three days completes the 'Marine List'. [ibid., p 76]

It is difficult in this age of world-wide radio and television, cables and telegraphs, cheap newspapers and general instant communication, to appreciate just how valuable these few bald facts were to people concerned with shipping in those days.

The next important development at the Coffee-House in Lombard Street was the appearance of *Lloyd's Register of Shipping*. There is some uncertainty about the date of this event, but evidence points to 1760, though the earliest Register surviving is dated 1764–6. It is described as follows:

The twelve printed columns of this Register contain 1) Former name (if any) of the ship; 2) Present name; 3) Master; 4) Port; 5) Port of Destination; 6) Tons; 7) Guns; 8) Men; 9) Date and Place of building; 10) Owner or Owners; 11) and 12) Letters showing condition of ship and equipment in 1764 and 1765 respectively. A final column headed '66' is left blank, to be filled in, in manuscript, for that year. In the column for guns, certain other particulars are frequently added, such as 'Sd B,' single deck with tier of beams. In the Classification columns the letters A, E, I, O and U give the state of the hulls, and G, M, and B (i.e., 'good,' 'middling,' and 'bad') the state of the equipment. Altogether, particulars of about 1,500 vessels are given. [ibid., p 86]

Then in 1769 Thomas Fielding, one of the waiters at the original Coffee-House,

Former	Present	Master	Port	To Port	Ton²	Guns	M	Built & Year	Owners	64	65	66
25	**D**											
	Daking —	Wm. Taylor	Lond.	Cork —	150	S D Bb	12	Liverp. 60	Daking & Co	E M	E M	
	Dalrymple	James Berry	Liverp.	Old Cl. & Am.	140 s	4	B 35	French 57	Davenport		E M	
	Dankbarhey	Cos Mandertz	Lond.	Amsterdam	160	S d	8	Amsterd. 62	Feitama	A G	A G	
	Dant. Packet	Hoisley		Riga —	200		11	River 54	Belford	E M		
	Darby —	Ist Boardman		Dublin —	80	S D	7	Plantation 61	J. Boardman			
Gen. Pact	Darlington	M'Lauglin		Quebec —	200	S D B B	12	River 56	P. Weathrall	E M	E M	
	David & Eliz.	John Brown		Rotterdam—	90 .	S L	8	Colchester 62	David Baker		A G	
	Dawes —	John Forbes		Jamaica	300 s	6	3 22	Ipswich 63	H. Mure	A G		
	Dawkins —	R. Ballentine		Mad. & Jam.	250 s	4	4 20	River 49	Alex. Grant	E M		
	Dean —	Jno Salisbury		Dublin —	130		12	Chester 50	John Dean			
Neptune	Dear Bessey	B. Beale	Liverp.	Cork & Barb	90 s		B 8	Plantation 56	Doran & Co.	E M		
	Deep Bay	Wm. Oliver	Lond.	St. Kitt's	180		13	62	J. & J. Mills	A G		
	Deep Bay	S. Dashwood		Boston —	150		B 10	Boston 63	Lane & Booth	A G		
	Defiance —	Shutter	Liverp.	Larne —	50		B 6	British 60		E M		
	Degartiquert	Rettine	Lond.	Hamburgh	100		5	Amsterd. 61	Rettine			
Jupiter	Delaware —	J. Jolly		Nap. & Mess.	300 s 16		2 32	Plantation 62	J. Jolly			
	Delaware —	Pet. Creaton			150		10	Philadel. 61	Wharton	A G		
	Delight —	W. Richards	Liverp.	Bon. & Am.	120 s		20	French 56	Rumbold & C	E M		
	Delight —	R. Barham	Yarm.	Naples	130	S d B	8	Yarmouth 53	Wm. Fisher	A G		
Matthew	Denia Castle	John Irwin	Lond.	Streights —	100	B	9	Plantation 60	C. Conner	A M		
	Devonshire	H. Hunter		Boston —	160		10	Boston 61	John Roe	A M		
Reaves —	Devonshire	Rich. Ashton		PtGreBs&We	200 s 8		4 15	French 58	Lewis Tesier	E M		
	DeVrowJoa	Pet. Smidt		Amsterdam -	200		12	Amsterd. 53	Tiddiman	E M		
Gen' Frd	Diadem —	Evan Johnson		Leghorn —	364 s 8		6 20	French 50	Tivitoe & C.	E M		
	Diamond —	Wm. Stott		Gen. & Leg.	280	16	4 32	River 41	Franco	E G		

23 A page of *Lloyd's Register* for 1764–6

set up a rival establishment, and on 18 March inserted the following notice in the *Public Advertiser*:

> To the Merchants in general, Owners, and Freighters of Ships, Insurance Brokers, &c &c THOMAS FIELDING, Waiter, from Lloyd's Coffee-house, begs leave to acquaint them, that his House in Pope's Head Alley, Lombard Street, is now genteely fitted up, and will be opened for the Reception of Gentlemen, Merchants, &c Tomorrow, the 21st Instant, by the Name of New LLOYD'S COFFEE HOUSE where he hopes to receive their favours, which shall be gratefully acknowledged, by
>> Their most obliged humble Servant,
>> Tho. Fielding.   [quoted ibid., p 102]

The two Coffee-Houses, each publishing its own *Lloyd's List*, continued in fierce competition for some years; but Fielding had taken with him the most solid of the underwriters, merchants, and shipowners and this gave the new house the bulge because

> ... it is not, after all, to the proprietors, but to the frequenters of Lloyd's Coffee House, that the Lloyd's of to-day can trace its origin. The merchants and underwriters who followed Fielding to Pope's Head Alley were the soul of Lloyd's Coffee House as a business institution. ...   [ibid., p 108]

In 1771 79 of these highly reputable and extremely solvent businessmen clubbed up 'for the building a New Lloyd's Coffee House', and three years later on Saturday, 5 March 1774 the move was made from Pope's Head Alley to premises over the north-west corner of the Royal Exchange, and Lloyd's, as distinct from Lloyd's Coffee-House, was finally and durably established.

There was always a great deal of money to be made in marine insurance. One famous underwriter, Richard Thornton by name, operating around 1800, left over £4 million. Nevertheless, the risks were high, especially in the period of incessant wars.

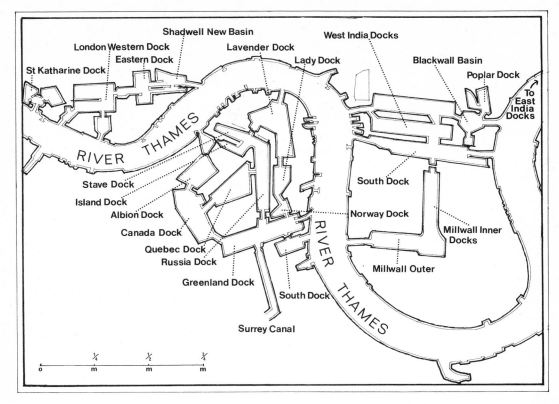

MAP NO. 9   The London Dock system

In 1782, for instance, the premium on a voyage from London to Jamaica was 12 per cent with convoy and 20 per cent without, and even at that a man could lose out. The greatest disaster ever to hit the underwriters was the loss of the Smyrna fleet in 1693 when 400 merchant ships bound for the Levant were attacked in the Bay of Lagos by the French and 100 of them, with cargoes valued at a total of £1 million, were captured or destroyed. Again in August 1780 a combined convoy of East and West Indiamen outward bound was attacked by a Spanish fleet and 55 out of the total of 63 ships captured. That day cost the underwriters at least £1½ million; but spreading the loss took the burden off the shoulders of both shipowners and merchants, which is precisely what marine insurance is about. And marine insurance as practised at Lloyd's was one of the background prerequisites for the expansion of the carrying trade that was to come.

2

Another essential was docks, especially in London, which as already demonstrated was by this time and remained for many years to come the very centre of world trade and shipping.

    The first wet basin in the Port of London was constructed as part of the Blackwall Yard, famous as the birthplace of those Indiamen known as *Blackwall Frigates*. Deepened and enlarged, it became the Poplar Dock and as such is still in use. However, towards the end of the 18th century, with the increase in the size of ships, the facilities afforded were no longer adequate and in 1789 the yard constructed another dock, officially

55

named the Brunswick as a compliment to the monarch, but popularly known as Perry's after the owner. The Brunswick Dock consisted of two basins, each with its own access to the river, and big enough to berth, in the larger, 30 first-class Indiamen and in the smaller, 30 lesser vessels. A famous feature of the dock was the masthouse; this structure was used for stepping the masts in Indiamen built or repairing in the yard, and in *Chronicles of Blackwall Yard* it is recorded:

> The first ship masted here on the 25th October 1791 was the *Lord Macartney*, East Indiaman. The whole suit of masts and bowsprit were raised and fixed in three hours forty minutes.　　　　　　　　　　　[quoted Millicent Rose, *The East End of London*, p 74]

From the same source comes the following glimpse of that famous yard in action at the beginning of the 19th century:

> April 1st, 1801: The *Agressor*, *Archer* and *Bold*, of 12 guns and 177 tons, were contracted for with the Government at £18 a ton. It was agreed that 5s. a ton extra should be paid on these vessels for every week that they should be completed within the contract time of four months. The *Agressor* was completed in 11 weeks and 3 days, the *Archer* in 11 weeks and 4 days, and the *Bold* in 13 weeks and four days.

　　In the beginning it was not merely for convenience of berthing or even the handling of cargo that the docks were built, but for protection. Under laws dating from Elizabethan times ocean-going vessels were compelled to moor in the river and discharge into lighters which then conveyed their cargo to licensed quays up-stream. This laid the ships open to both pilfering and smuggling on a grand scale, and all efforts to check them failed. Consequently, when the concept of wet-docks was accepted, they were built like fortresses 'defeating would-be offenders against private property and the Department of Customs and Excise'. They had high encircling walls with few gates, all small and very carefully guarded, and one of them – the West India – also had 'a moat or dug ditch, and a cleared space beyond in which an escaping thief would be uncomfortably visible'. The warehouses inside the ring of these walls matched up.

24　Brunswick Dock, by W. Daniell (1769–1837). Note masthouse in operation

They took the place of the keep, the stronghold within a stronghold, where tobacco and silks and spices, teas and wines were guarded more jealously than a Baron's wealth.

[ibid., p 126]

The West India was in fact the first, after the Brunswick. It was begun in 1800 and completed in 1802. Then came the London Docks, 1802–5, and the East India Docks, 1804–6, and this complex sufficed for 20 years after which the St Katharine Docks were built under the shadow of the Tower, with Tower Bridge itself still undreamed of.

— 3 —

And after the docks came the ships to use them.

A name to conjure with in regard to ship design in this period was Robert Leppings, Surveyor of the Navy. Refusing to be bound by tradition, to accept anything at all simply because it had always been so, he was remarkably uninhibited in his thinking and went some way to solving the ancient problem of hogging. His most important contribution was the introduction of diagonal ties and riders into the conventional pattern of transverse frames; but he also used 'filling pieces' in the spaces between the frames up to the bilges, which not only added longitudinal strength, but reinforced the ship's bottom and greatly reduced damage in the event of her stranding or when she took the ground, as ships often did in those days when most harbours were still open to the tides. Leppings also had something to do with the improvement of hull design. He reduced the size of the traditional beak-head and abolished high-square sterns from the Navy altogether. It might well be he was the first to realise that a ship's stern was not just something that followed willy-nilly after her fore-end, that the height, shape, and size of it had a direct and very important bearing, not only on her steering but also on her speed and general seaworthiness.

This was the time when the East Indiaman reached its zenith and the Honourable East India Company the peak of its prestige. Lubbock lists the following first-class ships built for the Company by the Blackwall Yard in the decade following the Napoleonic Wars:

1813: *Lady Melville* (1321 tons);
1816: *Waterloo* (1325 tons);
1817: *Canning* (1326 tons); *Duke of York* (1327 tons); *Thomas Coutts* (1334 tons);
1818: *Kellie Castle* (1332 tons);
1820: *Repulse* (1333 tons); *Royal George* (1333 tons); *Kent* (1332 tons);
1821: *Duchess of Athol* (1333 tons);
1824: *Surat Castle* (1223 tons);
1825: *Abercrombie Robinson* (1325 tons); *Edinburgh* (1325 tons).

[*The Blackwall Frigates*, p 37]

In addition to these big ships, the yard built in 1824 the *Simon Taylor* (408 tons); the *Lord Amherst* (506 tons); and the *Carn Brae Castle* (570 tons), the last one being specially designed for the Calcutta passenger trade.

By this time Sir Robert Wigram had retired, selling one half share in his Blackwall estate to a George Green and the other to two of his sons, Money Wigram and Henry Loftus Wigram. Green seems to have provided the driving force and the controlling

25 A West Indiaman in Cox & Curlin's Yard, Limehouse.

hand, and 1824 is also notable as the year when he acquired on his own account the *Sir Edward Paget* and with her started the Green Line of passenger ships to Calcutta. A year later he built the *Roxburgh Castle* (565 tons), and chartered her to John Company; and thereafter the name Green looms large in the history of sailing ships.

So the East Indiaman in the top class was now upwards of 1,200 tons; she mounted 26 guns and carried a crew of 130 all told. With this lavish manning, she was run like a man-of-war and her officers had the same social status as those in the Royal Navy. Indeed, everybody in an Indiaman, from the master down to the greenest deck-boy, thought himself somebody and competition for berths was fierce with string-pulling and nepotism rampant.

Of course not all ships were Indiamen or built at Blackwall. There were other yards on the London river – notably Wells' Yard at Deptford and Cox and Curlin's Yard at Limehouse – and shipwrights were practising their art in every port in the kingdom from Glasgow round south about to Dundee. They were building now at a great rate in Bombay and Calcutta – wonderfully slow ships, but solidly built of teak and virtually everlasting – and the Americans along the New England coast, after starting fairly small on slavers and whalers, were becoming more ambitious and challenging all comers for a share of the East Indies and China trade as well as on other profitable routes.

But none of them could touch the Indiamen for elegance, comfort, or performance. The *Thomas Coutts*, for example, which crossed three skysail yards, once made a voyage to China via India and back 'in ten days less than a year', doing the first leg from the Channel to Bombay in 82 days.

There was still a lot to be done, however, before the fruits of the newly won empire could be garnered, let alone enjoyed. Most of all, the cost of the long wars had to be met and by 1820 the charges arising out of the National Debt were absorbing almost three-fifths of Britain's tax revenue; £30 million out of a total of £53 million. And the money involved was the least part of it.

> Manufacturers had assumed that the ending of the war would at once throw open a vast market for their wares and had piled up stocks accordingly. Instead, there was an immediate fall in the demand for manufactured goods. . . .   [Morton, op. cit., p 353]

In 1815 both exports and imports fell. The price of iron declined from £20 to £8 a ton; three out of every four blast-furnaces in Shropshire went out of production and there was widespread unemployment among miners and iron-workers; and on top of all this over 300,000 demobilised soldiers and seamen were adrift in the country looking for work.

Another thing holding up the breakthrough was the struggle to suppress the slave trade: '. . . after the fall of Napoleon', writes J. Holland Rose, 'the greatest of all maritime issues was the suppression of the Slave Trade, which deeply concerned the extension of law and order over the oceans' (op. cit., p 241). The first Act abolishing the trade in English ships became law in 1807; but the penalties for breaking it were fines which the traffic could generally well afford to pay and still show a profit; and in 1811 another Act was passed, imposing the penalty of transportation. This was more effectual and over 150 British ships, most of them out of Liverpool, Bristol, and London, were 'put out of action by this reform'. That was the end of the Triangular Trade, but Britain's loss was America's gain, for although Congress in 1820 passed a law declaring slaving to be piracy and punishable with death, it was impossible to enforce it; and in the words of Judge Story of the American Supreme Court that same year: 'the African Trade is still carried on with the implacable ferocity and insatiable rapacity of former times' (quoted ibid., p 242). It was not until the second half of the century in fact that African slaving was finally stamped out; and for 50 years after the first Act of Abolition, the fight against it diverted valuable resources and held up progress.

The Barbary pirates were also a drag, working such havoc on shipping and along the coasts of the Aegean Islands that in the end the inhabitants took to the mountains out of fear of them and the Mediterranean basin was not made safe for the seafarer until France captured Algiers in 1830 and annexed the hinterland.

26   *Thomas Coutts* (1817), 1,334 tons, entering Bombay Harbour, by W. J. Huggins (1781–1845)

Finally, John Company itself, for all its magnificence, its wonderful ships, and enormous prestige – and in spite of the vast profits those involved in it were still making – had become in some ways a barrier to progress. Its privileges and especially its trading monopoly belonged to the past. It 'was a trading company, drawing most of its revenue from the profits derived from the sale in England of the exotic products of the East' (Morton, op. cit., p 447). As already noted, most of the outward cargoes the Indiamen carried were made up of silver – bullion or specie – and the British manufacturers' goods were largely left at home stacked in the warehouses. Something had to give, and in 1813 the East India Company's trading monopoly was abolished. The effect was dramatic.

> From this time can be dated the opening of the Indian market to English factory-made goods, above all to Lancashire-made cotton cloths. In a little over a decade the value of exports to India practically doubled, and the export of cotton goods, trifling in 1813, reached nearly £2,000,000 a year in the twenties. [ibid.]

27 Thomas Clarkson (1760–1846), the great philanthropist,
addresses the Anti-Slavery Society Convention in June 1840
in London

28 Capture of slaver *Borboleta* by boats of H.M.S. *Pantaloon*

And there was inevitably a tragic side to this development. Always somebody has to go to the wall and here it was the people of India. The machine-made Lancashire cottons virtually destroyed the hand-loom industry of the sub-continent and in 1835 Dr Bowring, a Member of Parliament and an advocate of Free Trade, declared:

> Some years ago the East India Company annually received of the produce of the looms of India to the amount of from six million to eight million pieces of cloth. The demand gradually fell off to somewhat more than one million pieces and has now nearly ceased altogether. . . . The Dacca muslins, celebrated over the whole world for their beauty and fineness, are almost annihilated from the same cause.

> [speech in Parliament, quoted ibid., p 448]

Dacca was the main centre of the Indian textile industry and between 1815 and 1837 its population decreased from 150,000 to a mere 20,000, most of whom were on the verge of starvation.

But although the writing was on the wall for them, this was by no means the end of the East India Company. They were powerful enough to ride the blow, and besides there were other monopolies, notably of the China tea trade, which they continued to enjoy for another 20 years. The value of this cargo on the London market was around £4 million a year now, and as the Company were selling it for roughly twice what it cost them in Canton it was well worth the trouble.

The Indiamen in this period were breathtaking in their beauty, so near to perfection, and so wonderfully functional. The *Earl of Balcarres*, for example. She was built of teak in John Company's own dockyard at Bombay in 1815 and she was big for her time – 1,417 tons. Lubbock lists her ship's company as:

29   July 1830. The French attack on Algiers

Commander	master-at-arms	2 bosun's mates
6 mates	armourer	2 gunner's mates
surgeon	butcher	2 carpenter's mates
assistant surgeon	baker	1 cooper's mate
6 midshipmen	poulterer	1 caulker's mate
purser	caulker	6 quarter-masters
bosun	cooper	1 sailmaker
gunner	2 stewards	7 officer's servants
carpenter	2 cooks	78 seamen

[*The Blackwall Frigates*, p 43]

A total of 130 all told. In 1831 the India husbands, tipped off that the Company's charter was expiring three years later, began selling their ships, but the *Earl of Balcarres* did not come into the market until September 1834 when she was bought in by Joseph Somes for £10,700. Two years later she was still good enough to make the passage to

61

Bombay in 79 days, and after over 50 years in the carrying trade she finished up as a hulk on the West Coast of Africa.

The scope of the East India Company's operations even at as late a date as 1830 is shown by the following notice in the shipping papers of that year:

East India Shipping Notice

On the 15th of May a Court of Directors was held at the East India House, when the following ships were taken up, viz:–

Duke of York, *Scaleby Castle*, *Warren Hastings*, *Kellie Castle*, *Buckinghamshire*, *Castle Huntly*, and *Vansittart*, for Bengal and China.

The *Marquis of Huntly*, *Duke of Sussex*, *Herefordshire*, *Farquharson* and *Lady Melville* for Bombay and China.

The *Waterloo*, *Thomas Grenville*, *Minerva*, and *Prince Regent*, for China direct.

Captain Bryan Broughton of the ship *Earl of Balcarres* took leave of the Court previous to departing for China direct.

[quoted ibid., p 42]

It was the year following this that the *Thames* (1,425 tons) made her famous fast passage from China, sailing on 18 November 1831 to pass Java Head on 5 December, St Helena on 28 January 1832, and arrive off Portland on 13 March, just 115 days out.

Lubbock describes the *Thames* as a typical first-class Indiaman of the last years of the East India Company. She was noticeably broad-beamed for her length and everything about her seemed ponderous – round bows, heavy stern, channels like great platforms, nine shrouds to her lower rigging, and both fore- and main-mast double stayed. The windows in her stern – 18 in all – were in two tiers with a narrow walk round the top one. Reading this description one is left marvelling at the passages she made.

30 East Indiaman *Earl of Balcarres*, 1,417 tons, built in Bombay, 1815

It is difficult to look beyond the Indiamen in this period, but there were other ships and other trades, some of which are incredible now. One such was the traffic from Boston round Cape Horn to California – not for gold or even silver, but simply for raw-hides. The details of this trade are recorded in R. H. Dana's *Two Years before the Mast*, than which no finer book about seafaring has ever been written. Dana sailed from Boston as a foremast hand aboard the brig *Pilgrim* in August 1832 and arrived off the Californian coast 150 days later. He then spent 18 months man-handling hides in the ship while she trundled up and down the coast and finally transferred to the ship *Alert* for the passage home, which took 137 days. He referred to his book as *a voice from the forecastle*, and this is precisely what it is – the first ever and still the most authentic. Of seafaring in his day he says:

> An overstrained sense of manliness is the characteristic of seafaring men, or rather, of life, on board ship. This often gives an appearance of want of feeling, or even of cruelty. From this, if a man comes within an ace of breaking his neck, and escapes, it is made a joke of, and no notice must be taken of a bruise or a cut, and any expression of pity, or any show of attention, would look sisterly, and unbecoming a man who has to face the rough and tumble of such a life. [p 215]

He and his shipmates made their own hard-weather clothes, cutting jackets and trousers out of a bolt of twilled cotton, then sewing them up with home-made sinnet and coating them thickly with linseed oil for water-proofing. Hats were made the same way and to keep out the cold they made up flannel underclothing. Their quarters in the forecastle were cramped, airless, dark, and damp and their food coarse beyond belief:

> The customs as to the allowance of 'grub' are very nearly the same in all American merchantmen. Whenever a pig is killed, the sailors have one mess from it. The rest goes to the cabin. The smaller live stock, poultry, etc., they never taste. And, indeed, they do not complain of this, for it would take a great deal to supply them with a good meal; and without the accompaniments (which could hardly be furnished to them) it would not be much better than salt beef. But even as to the salt beef, they are scarcely dealt fairly with, for whenever a barrel is opened, before any of the beef is put into the harness-cask, the steward comes up, and picks it all over, and takes out the best pieces (those that have any fat in them) for the cabin. . . . By this arrangement the hard dry pieces, which the sailors call 'old horse' come to their share. . . . [ibid., p 243]

But although he afterwards practised law, Dana was no *sea-lawyer*, and always he is recording rather than complaining. His description of the foremast hand rigged to go ashore even has a kind of gaiety about it:

> . . . . The usual outfit of pumps, white stockings, loose white duck trousers, blue jackets, clean checked shirts, black kerchiefs, hats well varnished, with a fathom of black ribbon over the left eye, a silk handkerchief flying from the outside jacket pocket, and four or five dollars tied up in the back of the neckerchief, and we were 'all right.' [ibid., p 199]

His second ship, the *Alert*, was a great improvement on the first. She had made the passage from Boston to Callao in a little over 80 days – one of the fastest times on record – and altogether she was bigger and better run. Her forecastle was large and reasonably well lighted, besides being kept scrupulously clean and dry; and she had 'tween decks 'as high as the gun-deck of a frigate', holystoned regularly and kept in the most perfect order. Part of the crew slept here in hammocks swung fore and aft from the beams; and here too were the carpenter's bench, the sailmaker's table, and the bosun's locker. Dana records that sometimes she would do 'eight or nine knots on a wind'. There was 'more room, more hands, more life . . .' than aboard the brig and at one point he cries out: 'Give me a big ship!' His description of her under full sail – a condition in which he declares very few people have ever seen a ship – is unbeatable:

> One night, while we were in these tropics, I went out to the end of the flying jib-boom, upon some duty, and having finished it, turned round, and lay over the boom for a long time, admiring the beauty of the sight before me. Being so far out from the deck, I could look at the ship as at a separate vessel – and there rose up from the water, supported only by the small black hull, a pyramid of canvas, spreading out far beyond the hull and towering up almost, as it seemed in the indistinct night-air to the clouds. The sea was as still as an inland lake; the light trade-wind was gently and steadily breathing from astern; the dark blue sky was studded with the tropical stars; there was no sound but the rippling of the water under the stem, and the sails were spread out, wide and high – the two lower studding-sails stretching on each side far beyond the deck; the topmast studding-sails like wings to the topsails; the topgallant studding-sails spreading fearlessly out above them; still higher, the two royal studding-sails, looking like two kites flying from the same string, and, highest of all, the little sky-sail, the apex of the pyramid, seeming actually to touch the stars and to be out of reach of human hand. So quiet, too, was the sea, and so steady the breeze, that if these sails had been sculptured marble, they could not have been more motionless. Not a ripple upon the surface of the canvas, not a quivering of the extreme edges of the sail – so perfectly were they distended by the breeze. I was so lost in the sight, that I forgot the presence of the man who came out with me, until he said (for he, too, rough old man-of-wars'-man as he was, had been gazing at the show), half to himself, still looking at the marble sails – *'How quietly they do their work!'*   [ibid., pp 280–1]

Also memorable is his description of the battle homeward round the Horn and particularly one piece of routine work while they were still on the wrong side of the Cape after 80 days of constant easterly gales. Occasionally the wind would haul a little to the southward and allow them to steal a little easting. But

> One night, after one of these shifts of the wind . . . it came on to blow worse and worse, with hail and snow beating like so many furies upon the ship, it being as dark and thick as night could make it. The mainsail was blowing and slatting with a noise like thunder, when the captain came on deck and ordered it to be furled. . . . Accordingly we went upon the yard; and never shall I forget that piece of work. Our watch had been so reduced by sickness, and by some having been left in California, that, with one man at the wheel, we had only the third mate and three besides myself to go aloft, so that, at most, we could only attempt to furl one yard-arm at a time. We manned the weather yard-arm, and set to work to make a furl of it. Our lower masts being short, and our yards very square, the sail had a head of nearly fifty feet, and a short leach made still shorter by the deep reef which was in it, which brought the clew away out on the quarters of the yard, and made a bunt nearly as square as the mizen royal yard. Besides this difficulty, the yard over which we lay was cased with ice, the gaskets and rope of the foot and leach of the sail as stiff and hard as a piece of suction hose, and the sail itself about as pliable as though it had been made of sheets of sheathing copper. It blew a perfect hurricane, with alternate blasts of snow, hail, and rain. We had to fist the sail with bare hands. No one could trust himself to mittens, for if he slipped he was a gone man. All the boats were hoisted in on deck, and there was nothing to be lowered for him. We had need of every finger God had given us. Several times we got the sail upon the yard, but it blew away again before we could secure it. It required men to lie over the yard to pass each turn of

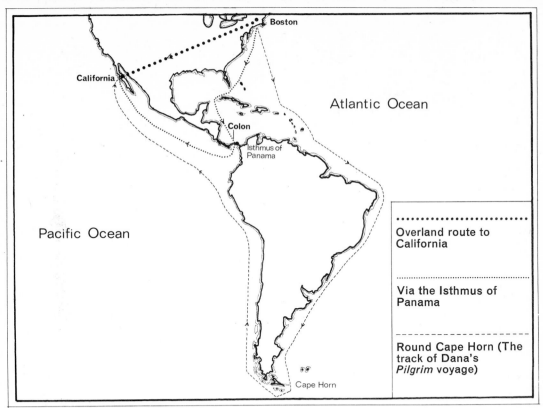

MAP NO. 10   The three routes to the Californian goldfields

the gaskets, and when they were passed, it was almost impossible to knot them so that they would hold. Frequently we were obliged to leave off altogether, and take to beating our hands upon the sail, to keep them from freezing. After some time, which seemed for ever, we got the weather side stowed after a fashion, and went over to leeward for another trial. This was still worse, for the body of the sail had been blown over to leeward; and as the yard was a-cock-bill by the lying over of the vessel, we had to light it all up to windward. When the yard-arms were furled, the bunt was all adrift again, which made more work for us. We got all secure at last, but we had been nearly an hour and a half upon the yard, and it seemed an age. . . .   [ibid., pp 272–3]

The enormity of the task can be better gauged by noting that these five men were tackling a sail with 'just half as many square yards of canvas in it as the mainsail of the *Independence*, a sixty gun ship, which musters seven hundred men at her quarters'. This was what the seafarer rightly called *man-killing*; and all for a cargo of 40,000 stinking raw-hides! The sea has been a lure since time began and the wonder is not that men let themselves in for such hazardous and heart-breaking labour, but that having experienced it once they should come back again and again for more. It certainly was not for the money they did it; the foremast hand by this time was earning little more than the price of a week or so of phoney high-living between voyages lasting up to a couple of years out and home.

Dana's descriptions of the Californian coast – sparsely populated with a handful of Spanish missions and trading posts manned in the main by Kanakas, with San Francisco not yet conceived in the minds of the planners, let alone built, and behind that a whole vast continent east of the Rockies still unpeopled – unconsciously underline the vital

65

31 A convict settlement at Norfolk Island, in the Pacific
between Australia and New Zealand

importance of large-scale emigration and show how even as late as 1832 the world was still more or less marking time for it.

Nevertheless, the first trickles that were to grow into great waves of migrant people were now more easily discernible and there was not much longer to wait. In Europe efforts to solve the economic problems left in the wake of the war were bearing more and more heavily on the landless, the dispossessed, the poverty-stricken, and the passionate ones who didn't want anything but a little social justice. So all over the old countries people were moving nearer and nearer to the point of desperation, where uprooting oneself and family to take a chance overseas seemed a better bet than staying. For some there was no option. 'There were many bankruptcies in 1815' (Morton, op. cit., p 361); and the same author notes 'in only three years from 1827 more than 8,500 men and boys were convicted of offences against the Game Laws and of these a very high proportion were transported'. And there were other laws besides these for breach of which the penalty was transportation.

Australia, the newly discovered continent 'at the end of the world', and 'right off all the main trade routes', looked as good a place as any wherein to dump the anti-social, the awkward, and the dissident elements like the Tolpuddle labourers who refused to knuckle under; and Australia had been a penal settlement since 1786 during which time 'thousands of the worst and the best English people were transported there'. Transportation in effect was always for life because there was no passage home organised for the time-served convict and very few indeed were ever able to raise enough money for the return fare or even to work their way back.

In spite of the brutal treatment they received, many of them became self-supporting farmers and artisans when their sentences expired. Others escaped into the interior to become bandits and bushrangers. [ibid., p 457]

Running convict ships was a branch of the carrying trade almost as gruesome as slaving. It must also have been profitable. One owner – Joseph Somes, an India husband and numbered among the promoters of *Lloyd's Register* – in 1840–1 had **six** ships on it. They were chartered to the government for the purpose and Lubbock records their names, tonnage, and what Mr Somes was paid for the use of them:

Maitland (648 tons)	£5	0	0	per ton per voyage
Asia (536 tons)	5	9	0	
Eden (522 tons)	5	13	9	
Lord Lyndoch (638 tons)	5	14	0	
Mary Ann (394 tons)	6	4	4	
Mexborough (376 tons)	6	6	0	

[*The Blackwall Frigates*, p 87]

The relatively small size of these ships is particularly interesting and it is difficult to avoid the conclusion that Dana's raw-hides round the Horn would be a better ride. Lubbock's description of one seems to confirm it:

> There was no gilt work about her, no weird carvings round her ugly sawed-off stern, no scroll work to relieve her clumsy white figurehead. A flush-decked ship, her decks are overcrowded with unsightly white-leaded box-like erections, and as she rolls we can see iron gratings over her open hatchways. On her main deck a line of slouching human cattle parade slowly in Indian file, watched over by red-coated despots with muskets at the shoulder. A growl, as of wild beasts, and the clanking of chains are borne to us on the wind. . . .   [ibid., p 59]

Another trickle significantly increasing in the 1820s was the young blood going out to administer the consolidated Empire and man the newly established outposts of commerce. Finally, and in spite of all the dire penalties imposed by the Acts of Abolition, there was still the slave trade. Between 1818 and 1820, according to one authority, 95,817 negroes were imported into Havana and years after that there were still 177 slave-ships arriving in Cuba annually. But that was only part of it, and in 1837 Sir Thomas Fowell Buxton, after the most careful scrutiny of the statistics,

> . . . reckoned that some 150,000 Africans were annually imported into Brazil, probably as many into Cuba, and smaller but still considerable numbers into Buenos Ayres and Porto Rico, besides 15,000 into Texas. . . .   [J. Holland Rose, op. cit., p 248]

Condliffe ignores the slaves and the convicts but sums up the rest:

> A marked characteristic of investment in the first half of the 19th century was the degree to which it was associated with the emigration, temporary and permanent, of both organisers and skilled workmen.   [op. cit., p 207]

And as these many different kinds of people stared out from the decks of Indiamen, convict ships, and slavers they sometimes saw on the edge of the otherwise empty – and in their minds always alien – sea, a trail of smoke. It would look odd in those days, quite out of place, and discussing it would make a brief break in the boredom of a long sea-passage, but to them it was no more important than a patch of gulf-weed or a shoal of flying fish breaking from under the bows. To the seafarer in the carrying trade, however, it was a portent.

The Advent of Steam

THE SEAFARER HAS NEVER OBJECTED to pulling his weight. Indeed, in time of necessity he works himself to a standstill with a kind of starry-eyed eagerness and abnegation of self-interest that makes nonsense of government regulations and negotiated agreements. He likes his measure of legal protection and has fought hard to get it, but he never hesitates to come out from under it if and when the need arises. Nor has he ever lacked patience. The very fact that he was able to make passages like the 150 days of Dana's *Pilgrim* and remain sane is proof of that. Nevertheless, he could always do without the frustrations inevitably associated with weather and tide and he has never been any fonder of hard labour for its own sake than a self-respecting coalminer or farm-hand. So ever since he went into the carrying trade he has been looking for ways of escaping the tyranny of wind and current, and means to reduce the backbreaking toil of working a ship about the world. The sail released him from the oar at a very early stage, but it also made bigger ships and longer voyages possible. They in turn demanded bigger sails and more of them, and very soon he was back where he had started – sweating his guts out except when the wind was fair and strong, but not strong enough to blow the canvas out of its roping. At all other times his job has always been both arduous and hazardous.

The ancient Egyptians were apparently the first to try and do something about it, though not everybody agrees to them having this credit. The evidence for it, as for so much else in early history, is in surviving temple sculptures from which it has been assumed that they had a ship or ships which were driven by paddle-wheels turned by oxen stalled on board for the purpose. If such a vessel did exist, its range and capacity must have been very limited, and the fact that the reference to it is so slight and so vague argues that it had little success and a very short life. But whether the Egyptians got anywhere with their oxen or not there is no doubt at all that inventors and dreamers from a long way back in time had been trying to think up some mechanical means of propelling ships.

The first possibility of real progress came with the discovery of steam as a source of power, and it is said the first attempt to propel a floating vessel by it was made in Barcelona by Blasco de Garay in 1583. The record is silent about the outcome and one can only wonder whether he blew himself up or burnt the bottom out of his boat and sank without a trace.

After de Garay there was nothing much until 1707 when Denis Papin of Cassel made a steam-driven engine for pumping water and then tried to adapt it to propel a ship. He built a model which he called the *Fulda* to demonstrate his invention, but was never able to prove its qualities because the local boatmen destroyed it in the night. No doubt they had a superstitious dread of a man-made thing that proposed to defy the laws of nature, and there was also the age-old and instinctive resistance to progress in any shape or form; but what really got them going was the fear that Papin was going to put them out of business, and he was lucky to get out of the place alive.

Thirty years after Papin – in 1736 – an Englishman named Jonathan Hulls dreamed up a steam-engine for driving a tug-boat; but though he took out a patent for it, the thing never got off the drawing-board and there was another blank period which lasted till 1769. By this time the stationary steam-engine as such was pretty well established, though there were still problems about it to be solved. The first successful harnessing of steam-power had been achieved by Thomas Savery, who in 1698 came up with a pump that worked. This was a very crude affair and it was succeeded in 1711 by Newcomen's engine which used a piston, piston-rod, and beam to work a pump that was quite separate from it. The engine itself was a reciprocating one and described in the simplest terms consisted of a cylinder in which a piston was moved to and fro by steam under pressure, the steam being alternately admitted to and released from the cylinder by means of valves operated by valve gear from the piston mechanism. Leaving aside for the moment the difficulty of setting up a steam-plant on such an unstable base as a ship afloat, the immediate problems were low boiler pressure and high efficiency-loss from condensation. It was to be a long time before the first one was solved by water-tubes and super-heating, but James Watt got round the second by using a separate condenser which eliminated the temperature drop in the cylinder.

The next significant dates were 1769, when James Watt patented a single-acting steam-engine with his separate condenser, and 1782, when he brought out the first double-acting engine. The name of Watt is for ever linked with steam-power. Besides the separate condenser, he devised the *expansive* working of steam which eventually led to the development of compound engines, in which

> ... steam is partially expanded in a small high-pressure cylinder, and then passed to a receiver; from here it is admitted to a larger low-pressure cylinder, where the rest of the expansion takes place, finally exhausting to the atmosphere, or a condenser.
>
> [*Everyman's Encyclopedia*, vol II, p 579]

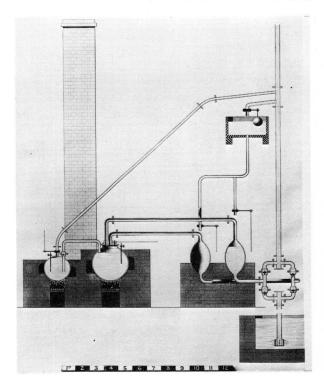

32 Savery's steam-
    pump

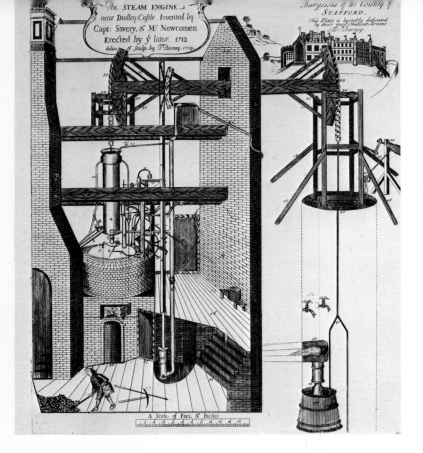

Other inventions of his fertile brain were lagging of cylinders and steam-pipes to prevent heat-loss, the stuffing-box to prevent steam escaping from the cylinder round the piston-rod, the governor, the indicator, and the parallel action out of which the modern cross-head and slide-bar evolved. He also invented the crank, but the patent was stolen.

In 1770 William Henry, an American, after seeing Watt's single-acting engine, experimented with a similar one in model boats. He was unsuccessful, but in 1786 James Ramsay built one that travelled up-stream at 4 miles an hour. This was the breakthrough, and four years later the American John Fitch had one doing 7 miles an hour. For all their success, however, Ramsay and Fitch were still mere experimenters, and it was not until 1802 that the first practical steamboat appeared. She was the *Charlotte Dundas*, built on the Forth and Clyde Canal by William Symington. In her he installed one of Watt's double-acting condensing engines which was linked through a crank-shaft with a paddle-wheel at the stern. She worked, towing 140 tons of cargo loaded into two barges behind her, but she was not allowed to do more than prove herself for fear, it was said, 'the wash . . . would seriously injure the banks'. Could be, of course, but one cannot help wondering whose toes Symington was treading on, what profitable business the success of the *Charlotte Dundas* appeared to threaten.

Checked thus in England, development shifted across the Atlantic where Robert Fulton, an early experimenter who knew Watt's engine and had seen the *Charlotte Dundas*, started building on his own account. In 1807 he launched the steamer *Clermont*. She did her first trip from New York to Albany, a distance of 150 miles, in 32 hours and returned in 30, which is as near 5 miles an hour for the round trip as makes no matter.

34 Watt's experimental steam-engine
with separate condenser. With this
apparatus he demonstrated the
invention patented in 1769. A. Outer
casing; B. Inlet to steam jacket;
C. Cylinder; D. Piston; E. Exit for
steam to condenser; F. Condenser;
G. Snifting valve, exhausting to
atmosphere; H. Air-pump cylinder

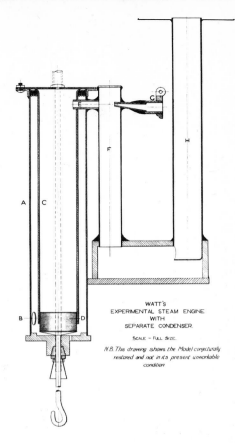

WATT'S
EXPERIMENTAL STEAM ENGINE
WITH
SEPARATE CONDENSER.

SCALE - FULL SIZE.

N.B. This drawing shows the Model conjecturally
restored and not in its present unworkable
condition

Encouraged by this success Fulton built two more steamers and set up a regular service.

The next to appear was the *Comet*, built in Scotland by Bell, Napier, and Robertson
and launched in 1812. This one was a 'side-wheeler' and could do a steady 6 miles an
hour. She too was an immediate commercial success and two others were built to work
along with her on the Clyde out of Glasgow.

The far-seeing had realised by now that steamships had come to stay and from this
time on, building them became an increasingly important industry on the banks of
the Clyde.

The first steamer to appear on the Thames was the *Marjory* in 1814, the first to
cross the open sea a vessel built by Napier for the purpose in 1818. She sailed between
Greenock and Belfast. Then in 1826 at Dover what was for those days a real giant of
a paddle-steamer was built. Bought by the Dutch as a man-of-war, she had a registered
tonnage of 438 and was first named the *Curaçao*. Within a year, however, she had been
renamed *Calpé* and set to carrying mails to the West Indies. She was the first-ever
steamer across the Atlantic, leaving Rotterdam in April 1827 and taking a month for
the passage.

The next big name in steamers was a Nova Scotian, Samuel Cunard. He had a
share in the building of the *Royal William*, designed and constructed in Canada to run
between Quebec and Halifax. In 1833 she was tried across the Atlantic and made the
passage from Quebec to London in 17 days which was wonderful going. Cunard's vision
must have been both powerful and insistent, for in 1838 he was in England himself for
the express purpose of establishing a regular mail service with steamships running from

Liverpool to Halifax and Boston. The builder he selected was Robert Napier, the famous Glasgow marine engineer, whose first brief was to build four steamships of over 1,100 tons. Cunard's project was backed by various British shipping interests, including George Burns of Glasgow and David MacIver of Liverpool, and between them they formed in 1839 the British and North American Royal Mail Steam Packet Company. And now, however deeply those who loved sailing ships or had money tied up in them might stick their heads in the sand and try to ignore the fact, the steamship had arrived and a battle that lasted the century out was joined.

All these early steamships were fitted with paddle-wheels. This meant that the main shaft was transverse – i.e. ran athwartships – at a considerable height above the ship's bottom and revolved slowly. The engine itself was of the side-lever variety which had been developed out of the beam engine used so successfully on land. The cylinder was bedded on the vessel's bottom and the lever at the side of it was driven by return rods from the cross-head. Those paddle-boxes must have been a terrible headache to the masters who were responsible for making safe passages in these ships. They were enormous excrescences. The *Forfarshire*, for instance, lost on the Farnes in 1838, was 40 feet 6 inches from side to side across the boxes and she was no more than 400 tons.

That same ship demonstrated in the most tragic way possible the fact that there were still many problems to be solved in the propulsion of ships by mechanical means and particularly in the marine boiler. Of course, great advances had been made since the first incredibly crude cast-iron box heated by a fire underneath; and again it was James Watt who had been largely responsible. He used wrought iron instead of cast and designed an internal flue which raised the effective pressure of the steam produced to 10 lbs. per square inch. In the *Forfarshire* the boilers were made of hand-riveted iron plates and designed to stand a pressure of 15 lbs. per square inch. But that was when they were new and at sea the iron corroded both constantly and at a rapid rate while the movement of the ship in a seaway was too much for the rivets. They worked loose and leaked with a consequent loss of pressure and of water that could be dangerous.

Until the late 1830s timber was still the shipbuilder's principal raw material and

35 Model of *Charlotte Dundas* (1802)

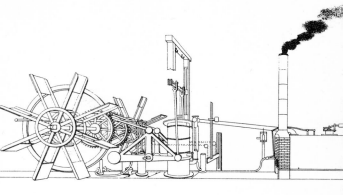

36 Robert Fulton's *Clermont* on the run
between New York and Albany,
1807

37 Machinery of Fulton's *Clermont*

the use of iron was largely confined to special cases and such tricky components as
brackets and elbows. This seems strange now when the advantages of metal over wood
are so obvious and particularly its weight for strength ratio. A wooden ship to be
reasonably seaworthy needed a construction so massive that she could lift very little
more cargo than her own weight; but one built of iron would carry twice that and the
smaller beams and frames taking up less room inside her would give appreciably more
cubic capacity for the overall dimensions. Yet there was a widespread reluctance to
change over. This prejudice against the use of iron in shipbuilding shows how foolishly
blinkered human beings – even otherwise intelligent ones – can be. Some of it, no doubt,
came from or was inspired by those with their money sunk in the timber trade and,
though their resistance was short-sighted, they can hardly be blamed for it in a world
where the most widespread occupation is *beggar-your-neighbour*. Then there were the
cranks, of course, who really believed that ships were built of wood because wood floated
and iron should not be used because it sank; but the majority of the resisters were not
even thinking it through. They resisted this change as they did any other, blindly and
instinctively, simply because it was change; they argued that ships had always been
built of wood and this, by some mysterious process of reasoning, meant they always
should and always would be.

And even though its habit of sinking in water was not one of them, there were
objective and valid arguments against the use of iron. There were difficulties in working
it for certain parts of a ship, limits to the shapes that could be imposed on it both as
plates and in the bar; it varied considerably in quality and above all in contact with
the sea it corroded at an alarming rate and quickly became foul with marine growth.
So, for one reason and another, in the beginning iron was used sparingly and the
reasonable objections to it were met by devising the *composite* ship – one constructed of
wooden planking on iron frames with copper sheathing to keep the bottom clean and
discourage the worms.

The first of the ships built by Napier for Samuel Cunard was a wooden steamer.
Her name was the *Britannia* and she is described as 'a wooden paddle steamer of
1,135 tons and 207 feet in length with a speed of 8·5 knots; she had accommodation for
115 passengers and could carry 225 tons of cargo' (*The Times*, 12 July 1965). These

38 Samuel Cunard (1787–1865)

39 James Watt (1736–1819). Mezzotint after Sir T. Lawrence (1769–1830)

figures show she carried an extraordinarily small amount of cargo for her size and it follows that most of her available cubic capacity was taken up by the provision of amenities for the passengers – cabins, dining-saloon, smoking-rooms, and other public rooms. She was a three-master and barque-rigged with a shapely bow and long bowsprit. Her paddles were on either side amidships with the funnel abaft them and just forward of the mainmast. The sailing ship was still the dominant element in her and she retained a great deal of the lovely shape that was the sailing ship's special pride.

The *Britannia* sailed from Liverpool on her maiden voyage on 4 July 1840 and made the passage to Boston in 14 days and 8 hours. She thus inaugurated a regular transatlantic mail service for the British government which Cunard had contracted to maintain for seven years at £60,000 a year. The agreement took in, besides Boston, both Halifax and Quebec.

But Cunard was by no means first in this trade. Two years before – and two years had suddenly become a long time in the carrying trade – on 5 April 1838 a steamer called the *Sirius* left Cork bound for New York, and 3 days after that the *Great Western*, a paddle-steamer 236 feet long with a 25-foot beam and 23 feet deep, sailed from Bristol for the same destination. She belonged to the Great Western Railway and was a flyer, taking 15 days only for the passage and making up 72 hours on the *Sirius*.

That year was also memorable for a ship called the *Rainbow*, the first-ever all-iron ship of any size in the world. She was built to trade between London, Ramsgate, and Antwerp and in spite of all the gloomy predictions she stayed afloat.

Nevertheless, as an iron ship the *Rainbow* was still a bit of an experiment. It might be all right to use such a vessel coastwise and in narrow waters, but trans-oceanic traffic was a different proposition. To build of iron for deep-water passages and finally break down the prejudice, put to scorn the traditional thinking, and override the vested

74

interests in timber ships, a man of vision was needed and, moreover, he had to have a gambler's nerve to be able to follow his vision through. And it was now that history produced that man. His name was Isambard Kingdom Brunel.

Brunel was an engineer. He was born at Portsmouth in 1806, son of another engineer, equally famous, Sir Marc Isambard Brunel. I.K. was a bright lad with a flare for mathematics and an inventive mind. At 14 he went to Paris to finish his formal education at the Collège Henri Quatre and at 17 started work in his father's office. Thereafter his life, though short – he was only 53 when he died – was singularly full of achievement. He built bridges, railways, docks, canals, and, above all, ships; and whatever he built, he made it big. From 1833 to 1846 he was the Chief Engineer of the Great Western Railway and as such he dreamed up and built the *Great Western*, the *Great Britain*, and the *Great Eastern*. Brunel's *greats* they might be called, and each of them was remarkable in some very special way.

To the *Great Western* goes the honour of being the first steamship to run a *regular* service between England and America, its regularity, of course, being the great thing and in those days remarkable in a way and to a degree that can no longer be appreciated. The *Great Britain*, launched in 1843, was the first ocean-going ship constructed entirely of iron and the first ever to be driven by a screw instead of side- or stern-paddles. Dr Euan Corlett, the eminent naval architect, has called her 'the forefather of all modern ships'. Built at Bristol, she had six masts, a single funnel, and her engines developed a phenomenal 1,000 horse-power. She was a long time fitting out and her maiden voyage was not made until August 1845 when she made the crossing to New York in 14½ days.

Brunel was not an inventor and the screw-propeller was not his brain-child; but he backed it as he did the iron ship and in the face of the same kind of opposition. The origin of the screw, in fact, like that of the wheel, is lost in antiquity but it was adapted for marine propulsion by John Ericsson. In 1836 he submitted his idea to the British Admiralty, but they believed a screw-propeller would tend to drive a ship in circles and no steering device could correct such a tendency and keep the ship on a straight course. Failing to convince them otherwise, Ericsson turned to the United States Navy Board which welcomed him with open arms and equally open minds. They got the back-room boys busy and presently they came up with a design for the first screw-propelled warship

40 *The Britannia* (1840), 1,135 tons, the first Cunarder

which was launched in 1843 and named the *Princeton*. It was planned to use her in the struggle to suppress the slave trade and a curious feature of her was telescopic funnels, whereby she could be disguised as a sailing ship and as such creep up on a suspect.

Meanwhile, in England Francis Pettit Smith had proved Ericsson's idea in an experimental ship which he launched in 1839 and named, appropriately, the *Archimedes*. It must have been this and the *Princeton* together that decided Brunel to gamble on the screw in the *Great Britain* for she was originally planned as a paddle-steamer. She was the most successful of his *greats* and is still afloat today (1968) as a hulk in Sparrow Cove near Port Stanley in the Falkland Islands. (Indeed, a scheme is afoot to tow her home to be restored and put on permanent show in Jefferies Dock, Bristol, where she was built.)

The success of the *Great Britain* shook the pundits of the Admiralty out of their complacency, but they still refused to admit they had been wrong to turn down Ericsson. The advantages of the screw were obvious now. Unlike the paddle-wheels, it was not affected by the rolling of the ship or even her pitching, provided she was well enough ballasted or deep enough loaded to keep the screw submerged; changes in draught caused less variation in speed, and above all a ship so propelled could take in her stride storms that would make matchwood and twisted iron scrap of both paddles and paddle-boxes. The screw-propeller was also *mechanically* more efficient than paddles, acting on a relatively larger volume of water in any given time. But the Lords of the Admiralty wanted more proof and in 1845 they staged an experiment on the Solent which was to settle the question once and for all. Two ships were concerned in it – H.M.S. *Rattler*, a screw-steamer, and H.M.S. *Alecto*, a paddle-steamer of approximately the same tonnage and horse-power. First they ran against each other in a series of speed and manœuvring trials which the *Rattler* won hands down; then linked with tow-ropes and heading in opposite directions they began pulling against each other, in a kind of tug-of-war. The result was that the *Rattler* finished up towing the *Alecto* backwards against the maximum thrust of her paddles at 2½ miles an hour. Convinced at last, the

41 Isambard Kingdom Brunel
      (1806–59)

42 The contest between H.M.S. *Rattler*
      (screw) and H.M.S. *Alecto*
      (paddles) in 1845

43   Brunel's *Great Eastern* (launched 1858)

Admiralty promptly ordered more than 20 ships to be fitted with screw-propellers, and paddles for deep water were on the way out. Five years later there were no fewer than 31 screw-steamers in the British Royal Navy, and on iron ships the famous builder, John Laird, declared that no private firm would thereafter build a wooden steamer.

Brunel's third and final *great* was the *Great Eastern*. She was built in London at the yard of John Scott Russell in Millwall, and from keel-laying to launch the job took three years. As a ship she was typical of all I.K.'s work and thinking – big and at least 50 years ahead of her time. Started in 1854, she was 692 feet long and Brunel gave her everything that was going – one set of engines driving 58-foot paddle-wheels, another working a 24-foot screw-propeller, six masts carrying 6,500 square yards of sail, and five funnels to take away the smoke from her boilers and supply their furnaces with an adequate draught. Maybe she was too big or too far ahead of her time, but either way disaster dogged her from the very beginning:

> During the years of her building, 1854–7, her phenomenal hull was the dominant feature of Millwall. Almost seven hundred feet long, she was too large to be launched in the usual way, and Brunel had her built broadside on to the river, into which he proposed to ease her sideways when the time came. On the day of the attempted launching, in November 1857, the directors acted against Brunel's wishes by selling thousands of tickets to watch the *Leviathan* (as she was at first to be called) move down her slipways and into the river. Hordes of sightseers milled about the shipyard, destroying the conditions of quiet upon which Brunel had depended, for his method of launching was based upon co-ordination between the many dozens of men who were to work in teams on the barges in the river and the windlasses ashore. Amid the press of sightseers, shouted commands became inaudible. The work began, the *Leviathan* moved a few feet and then stuck upon her rollers. A windlass rushing round with unexpected suddenness tossed a worker into the air and fatally injured him; a panic followed, and the bargemen in the river deserted their part of the task, for they feared that the great ship would come crashing down upon them. So the *Leviathan* remained high and dry on her cradles, hardly shifted from where she had been built; she was there for three months, the mock of every envious soul in London.
>
> [Millicent Rose, op. cit., p 147]

77

44   The Cunarder *Persia* (1856), 3,300 tons

She was finally launched on the last day of January 1858 and surrounded by fleets of small craft full of excursionists she was towed between banks lined with sightseers to Deptford for fitting out. This took another 20 months. Her maiden voyage began on 7 September 1859 and 8 days later Isambard Kingdom Brunel died without knowing what kind of a showing she had made. When it came to the reckoning she had cost too much to build and was too expensive to run ever to show a profit on the transatlantic run. Taken off it, she served for some years as a cable ship; then in 1888 she was permanently moored in Liverpool and after a few shameful months as a fun-fair broken up for scrap. There is some comfort in the thought that Brunel did not see the end she made.

In a way the *Great Eastern* sounded the death-knell of significant shipbuilding on the Thames:

> . . . the difficulties of her launching indicate one reason why, with the development of large iron ships, ship-building ceased to be an important East End industry. Besides the comparative narrowness of the Thames above Blackwall, there was another good reason: London was far from the sources of such raw materials as coal and iron. Nevertheless, the industry was carried on until 1867, by owners, unwilling to cease using shipyards which they had equipped with considerable expense.   [ibid., p 148]

During all this time Samuel Cunard had been increasing the size of his fleet and slowly extending his grip on the transatlantic passenger and mail-carrying trade. In 1847 the *Hibernia*, one of the *Britannia*'s three sister ships, established a toe-hold in the New York trade by calling at Jersey City, and in 1852 the Company built its first screw-propelled iron ship, the *Andes*.

Passengers in the *Andes* missed the great paddle-boxes. Paddles, like sails, were a visible symbol of power; seeing them it was easy to understand what was going on and just why and how the ship was moving from A to B. They gave a sense of security lacking in a ship driven – God only knew how – by an unseen screw reputed to have been invented by some Greek philosopher thousands of years ago. Absurd as this

78

attitude might seem today, Cunard had to come to terms with it then and did so in his next transatlantic flyer. She was the *Persia*, built in 1856. She too was an iron ship and at 3,300 tons the largest ship afloat, preceding Brunel's giant by three years. In her, says the Cunard Company,

> . . . the paddle wheel was retained. This was mainly because the travelling public cherished the visible assurance of a ship's power that was given by the paddle wheel as against the unseen screw propeller, much as a later generation liked to see an array of funnels. [*The Times*, 12 July 1965]

Contemporary pictures of her make her out to be quite a ship – long, flush-decked, and sitting low in the water. She had a clipper-bow and without the monstrous paddle-boxes amidships might have been a beauty. There were two funnels in her and she was brig-rigged. Her maximum speed was $12\frac{1}{2}$ knots.

By this time the shape of things to come was beginning to emerge and in 1862 Cunard abandoned the paddle, and that was virtually the end of it in deep-water ships. Meanwhile, boilers and engines had naturally developed to keep up with new hull design and methods of propulsion. By mid-century boiler pressures had been upped from the original 10 lbs. per square inch to first 60 and then 120, and this enormous advance led to the introduction in 1870 of compound engines. By this time, too, the methods and terms used in the measurement of ships had been standardised, making comparison of one with another more meaningful. Size could be indicated in three different ways:

(a) *Gross tonnage* – giving the cubic capacity of the ship calculated at 100 cubic feet to the ton.

(b) *Net tonnage* – giving the cubic capacity less the total volume of those spaces such as engine- and boiler-rooms, crew quarters, and stowage for stores not available for cargo. Dock, harbour, and other dues levied on ships are calculated from this measurement.

(c) *Deadweight* – giving the amount of cargo in long tons (i.e. of 2,240 lbs. each) a ship can lift fully loaded. Used particularly of cargo ships and bulk carriers like tankers.

All these things were important, pointing the way ahead and foreshadowing even greater advances still to come; but for the carriers, the really significant name in the middle decades of the century was not Brunel's *Great Eastern* nor Cunard's *Persia*; it was neither a ship nor a shipbuilder but a different kind of dreamer – a Frenchman called de Lesseps who had a passion for short cuts and in 1856 began digging a ditch across the Isthmus of Suez.

45 Ferdinand de Lesseps (1805–94)

The Golden Age

. . . by the middle of the century the foundations of British shipping
and commercial supremacy had been firmly laid.

[Condliffe, op. cit., p 207]

IN SPITE OF THE ALMOST INSTANT SUCCESS of steamships in the transatlantic passenger and mail service, and the great increase in their number coasting and running on the *home-trade* routes (defined as 'between Brest and the Elbe'), they had by no means swept the board when de Lesseps began digging in the Isthmus. Indeed, there were still many hard-headed shipping people who continued to look on steamers as a mere novelty as well as some, perhaps a little less concerned with profit and loss, who considered the stinking things sinful, a kind of sacrilege or blasphemy. Together they added up to a lot of people with money to invest in the carrying trade, who preferred to put it into something that looked the way a ship had always done in their experience. And apart from such more or less subjective reactions to the sight of funnels and the smell of frying engine-oil, there were very sound objective reasons for preferring sailing ships.

In the first place, a sailing ship was self-sufficient in a way a steamer never could be. With a coop-full of chickens tucked away in a sheltered spot on deck, a pregnant sow in the pig-sty, and a couple of years' supply of salt-meat stowed in barrels in the lazarette, a sailing ship could keep the high seas more or less for ever, so long as she was sheathed against the worm. Not so the steamer. Her engines required periodical maintenance work done on them, her boilers – even in the later, more sophisticated form – needed cleaning and scaling as well as frequent re-riveting and patching, and above all else she had to replenish her bunkers at frequent intervals.

Bunkers were a real problem. Of course, coal-mining had been a thriving business in England for centuries and it got going in a big way in America around 1820 when the Schuylkill Navigation Company started shipping coal down the Lehigh and Delaware rivers to Philadelphia, so the transatlantic steam packets were well provided for on both sides of the Ocean. But the further a ship got from these main sources of supply the more difficult the problem of bunkers became. The trouble was that every ton of coal carried meant that much less capacity for cargo and, though bunkering stations were quite soon established on the principal trade routes, stocks had to be shipped out to them, and the cost of coaling there rose steeply as the distance from the home port increased. This difficulty was never completely overcome for coal-burning steamers and a ship outward bound with bunker coal stacked high on her decks was a common sight well into the 20th century. Indeed, bunkers in some of the outports were so expensive that sometimes it was a worthwhile proposition deliberately to reduce the ship's outward cargo by stowing one hold with coal for the homeward passage; and cases of tramp-steamers running short of coal after encountering a long spell of head winds were quite common. The outcome of such a mischance was usually an unscheduled call to replenish the bunkers; but often enough this option was not open and she would have to burn anything combustible on board – derricks, hatch-covers, and even part of the cargo – to make port. This, of course, involved the owner in great expense and the favoured way of working off the consequent peeve was to sack the chief engineer and/or master. For them, running short of bunkers was a recurrent nightmare on long passages.

Steam-power had its greatest immediate impact on the slave trade. As already noted, the slavers used small, fast sailing ships designed for particularly good performance in light airs and going to windward. They got away with their cargoes largely because they were superior in this respect to the frigates and sloops detailed to capture them. But steam-power sprung the balance against them, and in February 1850 the Minister responsible was able to advise the House of Commons that '. . . our West African squadron had in 1840–8 captured 625 slavers, thus liberating 38,033 negroes . . .' (J. Holland Rose, op. cit., p 255). This was a severe set-back to the trade but, acting on the idea that what is sauce for the goose is equally effective for the gander, the slavers promptly went in for steam themselves. Indeed, some of them were already in it, for in March 1846 the brand-new steam-frigate *Penelope* captured a steamer with a cargo of 1,500 slaves on board. She was the *Cacique*, sailing under the Brazilian flag but American owned, and she was taken in port while completing her load. If the frigate had encountered her on the high seas, she may well have been the faster of the two and got away, and for a while there was a real possibility of this kind of stalemate developing – the slavers keeping just one jump ahead by building ships a knot or so faster than the fastest of the steam-frigates. But bunkers broke the impasse before it could really develop. The naval squadron had coaling stations established for it at Freetown and Sherboro', and after 1851 at Lagos itself. They were all right for coal, but the slavers had to bunker where they could and as the process took several days it made them extremely vulnerable. J. Holland Rose sums up the situation:

> . . . slaving steamers had very great difficulty in getting in coal on the African coasts. Even our steam cruisers, which could coal at our depots in Sierra Leone or at Fernando Po, took three or four days at a time; so we ought always to catch a slaver while coaling where there were no facilities. In truth in the age of steam then dawning, victory must crown the efforts of efficient steamers having good coaling stations near by. Also, as the slaver needed secrecy, she was heavily handicapped in having to repair to definite coaling-places.   [ibid., pp 225–7]

In spite of all this, however, the total abolition of the slave trade was not yet accomplished. When the issue was finally decided it was done in blood other than African and on battlefields far from the steaming jungles and mangrove swamps of the Guinea Coast.

For the sailing-ship designer, the advent of steam was at first a great blessing. It freed him from one of his most frustrating limitations. Hitherto, in dreaming up a ship he had to begin by trying to reconcile a number of mutually antagonistic factors. He wanted her big and he wanted her fast, and so long as she was out and away she could be more or less as big and as fast as he liked; but at the beginning of every passage there was a harbour to get out of and at the end of it another one to get into, while all over the world there were stretches of narrow water as well as rivers to be navigated. This meant he was restricted to a size and a rig which together added up to a ship capable of manœuvring in and out of port without assistance. But now with steam-tugs at river mouths and harbour bars to ease his ship out for her departure and pluck her in at the end of the deep-water passage, he could go the limit on size and pile his kites sky-high. As shall be seen, this was exactly what he did.

Among the big names in sail around the middle of the century was Brocklebank. The Company, now claimed to be the 'oldest line in the world', was founded in 1775 by Daniel Brocklebank, the son of a Cumberland parson. Daniel went to America and set up as a shipbuilder and shipmaster at Sheepscutt, Massachusetts. When the American War of Independence came, he had five ships operating and, deciding there was no future for him on that side of the Atlantic, he abandoned four of them and sailed for his Cumberland home aboard the fifth. She was the brig *Castor* (220 tons). The story goes that he got her away by the skin of his teeth and had no time to store her or to ship provisions for the crew; but being a resourceful man, he stopped on the Banks of Newfoundland and caught sufficient fish for the passage, salting it down with the scrapings off the ship's timbers. Arriving at Whitehaven on 8 June 1775, Daniel set up as a shipowner in that port. Most of his early trade was across the Atlantic, while his brother John chanced his arm in the Greenland whaling; but in 1813 the firm went into the Indian trade. Ventures to China followed and by 1850 they were all over the world with a fleet of 70 ships. Their outward cargoes were mostly Manchester bales and homeward they carried tea from China, jute and linseed from India, and copper ore from the west coast of South America.

Another famous firm was Rankin, Gilmour, and Company of Liverpool, whose fleet numbered 78 ships in 1824. Lubbock records they were shipping between 300 and 500 cargoes of Canadian lumber across the Atlantic each season in the 1830s, and in 1843 they had 60 ships hauling guano from the island of Icheboe off the West African Coast.

There were other owners besides these, of course; so many in fact that the sight of '300 sail held up in the Downs or the chops of the Channel by a long continuance of head winds' was not unusual; and generally speaking the sailing ship still had the bulge. She consumed nothing except food and water for her crew, and apart from stowage for these two items, every cubic foot of her capacity was available for pay-load. Looking back on the situation in the 1830s the wonder is that the steamer was ever able to establish itself at all. Up till then time for the carrier had been of little consequence. Dana's 150 days from Boston to California and the long voyages of the East Indiamen to China and back are proof of this. The mind that could consider the 115 days' passage of the *Thames* from China phenomenally fast and contemplate with equanimity round voyages lasting upwards of two years was not at all impressed by the odd day saved here and the few hours won back there. If he got head winds and made a long passage so what! The cargo would keep and he was running up no accounts but the wages bill which was low enough not to count anyhow. So for the seafarer, broadly speaking, the only advantage of the steamer – its ability to make passages in adverse weather conditions – hardly counted in the reckoning. But in the 1840s it was different, for then the trickles of people moving about the world became great migrating waves and time to them was everything that mattered.

There are many reasons for people emigrating – personal ambition, political and economic pressures, an itching foot, inability to adapt to changes in society, desire to escape the consequences of some folly or a situation no longer tolerable, and so on – and few ever do it for any single one of them. Almost invariably it is the cumulative effect of a man's objective circumstances working on his basic character that finally uproots him. He feels the urge and though he resists it, it stays with him, and he keeps on weighing the pros and cons until one day the balance is sprung and he books his passage. That

46 *The Last of England*
by Ford Madox
Brown (1821–93).
A Victorian view of
the emigrant

was the way of it for the millions of Europeans who left the land of their fathers during the second and third quarters of the 19th century. Some of the pressures working on them were purely personal and others too obscure or complex to be recognised with any certainty; but, broadly speaking, these people were all in one way or another, and in varying degrees, casualties of the Industrial Revolution. Among them were peasants forced off the land they had worked for generations and never owned, hand-craftsmen unable to compete against the new machines, small-scale producers squeezed out of business by the ever-growing factories using steam-power, and countless thousands who had nothing to trade with but their labour and could find no satisfactory market for it in Europe.

Yet it was a time of expansion. In 1823 the Stockton and Darlington Railway had been opened and six years later a line was working between Manchester and Liverpool. After that, the railway building boom set in, and in two years in the mid-1830s something like £70 million was raised for constructing new tracks. Quite soon there was an enormous network radiating from London and the main seaports, and an immense increase in manufacturing and in trade quickly followed.

Exports rose from £69,000,000 in 1830 to £197,000,000 in 1850, but more important than this mere quantitative increase was the stimulus given to certain key industries especially coal mining and iron. The output of pig iron was 678,000 tons in 1830; in 1852 it was 2,701,000 tons. Coal output rose from ten million tons in 1800 to one hundred million tons in 1865. [Morton, op. cit., p 388]

It was a fabulous age for some people, for others the blackest and most desperate in history, and nobody suffered in it more than the Irish. They had become a nation of corn-growers with an assured market in England protected by the Corn Laws, which kept the price high and prohibited imports from continental Europe and America. 'The peasant', says Morton, 'grew wheat to pay the rent and potatoes to feed himself and his family', and somehow he managed to get by. Then in 1845 the potato crop failed. This disaster was followed by five whole years of famine during which thousands died of starvation. The period also saw England repeal the Corn Laws in 1846 and the special market for wheat was gone overnight; with it went the very reason for the Irish peasant's existence and consequently another great exodus was on. As noted earlier, between 1841 and 1891, when everywhere else population was expanding, in Ireland it fell by $3\frac{1}{2}$ million.

This was one of the waves for the carriers. In the main it was headed west, but there were other destinations than the Americas. The colonisation of New Zealand had begun in 1837 and by 1840 the number of people voluntarily pouring into Australia had grown so much that plans for running down and abandoning the convict station there were got under way. But America was undoubtedly the promised land:

> Many emigrants went to Canada, while the building of railways in the United States (2,500 miles by 1840) opened vast new territories beyond the Alleghany Mountains. By 1840 about 70,000 people a year were emigrating. . . . [ibid., p 390]

The builders of sailing ships were not blind to the challenge of steam and, recognising that the leisurely days and stately ways of John Company's Indiaman were gone for ever, Green and Wigram had long since set about modifying her to meet the demands of the times. The result of their efforts was the *Seringapatam* (818 tons), launched in 1837 at the Blackwall Yard. She was the first of the Blackwall frigates. The

47   The *Seringapatam* (1837), 818 tons, off the Needles,
     by T. G. Dutton

biggest change about her, so far as appearance goes, was in her stern, the heavy double stern, and quarter galleries, so long a feature of the East Indiaman, being abandoned for an altogether lighter, cleaner structure. This modification produced a marked improvement in speed. A passage of 85 days from the Lizard to Bombay is not unusual in the record of her voyages and she was used as a model for many of Green's later ships. Among them Lubbock lists:

1837 *Madagascar* (835 tons). Lost without a trace on passage home from Melbourne in 1853
1838 *Earl of Hardwicke* (852 tons). Driven ashore on South African coast in 1866
1839 *Owen Glendower* (852 tons)
1839 *Vernon* (911 tons). Became a reformatory school ship at moorings in Sydney Harbour
1841 *Agincourt* (958 tons)

Still trying to build ships to match the growing demands the progress of history was making on the carriers, the Blackwall Yard made further modifications and in 1842 launched the *Prince of Wales* (1,223 tons), and the *Queen* (1,223 tons). 'At their launch,' says Lubbock, 'these two vessels were considered to be the finest examples of armed merchantmen that had ever been built' (*The Blackwall Frigates*, p 130). They could be described as multi-purpose ships, being pierced for 50 guns, specially fitted for carrying troops, and at the same time providing a ladies' boudoir for first-class passengers. The first thing about them to strike the eye was their size, for they were 179·4 feet long, 39·7 feet in the beam, and 22·9 feet deep. For the rest

. . . they were a return to the grandeur of the old John Company's East Indiamen. To modern eyes their 'tween decks would have appeared very low and dark, their bows very apple-cheeked, their channels vast platforms and their sterns, lumpy and heavy, yet these old frigates were by no means slow, especially in light winds.   [ibid., p 130]

As proof of their qualities, Lubbock quotes the *Prince of Wales* in 1860 'with a crew of 78 men and 120 passengers making the passage out to Hobson's Bay in 77 days' (ibid.).

In 1840 two more names become prominent in the records of shipbuilding and shipowning, the Tyneside firm of T. and W. Smith and Duncan Dunbar of Sunderland. Of the two, Dunbar was the more romantic figure. He began building of teak in Moulmein, Burma, and his ships were famous for their strength. The *Marion* (684 tons), launched in 1834, was many years in the North Atlantic trade before being wrecked off Newfoundland in 1877 and the *Lady Macdonald* (678 tons) was still afloat 30 years after she was built in 1847. Dunbar built and ran many famous ships in the Indian and Australian trades and when he died in 1862 he left a fortune of £1½ million.

There is no telling now how much of a spur this competition from the north-east coast builders was to the Blackwall Yard, but it is safe to assume it had some effect and, shedding more and more inhibitions on the way, Green finally produced the *Monarch* (1,444 tons). The following is a contemporary description of her:

The *Monarch* is 1400 tons burthen; length of keel 168 feet; length overall 180 feet; depth from upper deck to keelson 32 feet. The breadth of her beam is 40 feet, and it is only in this particular that she is inferior to the first-class frigates of H.M. Navy.
She has an entire flush deck fore and aft; is pierced for 50 guns, and capable of carrying a greater number, for besides 16 ports on a side upon the main deck there is also an equal number of large scuttles on the lower deck.

Her timbers and planking are chiefly of teak; the planks next the keel are American elm 5 inches thick, above this is teak to the whales, which are formed of African oak; the topsides are entirely of teak, and her bitts, capstan and most of the interior work are of the same wood.

There are 12 cabins, averaging 11 feet by 10 each, and a dining-room 36 feet by 18 feet on the main deck, the forepart of which is bulkheaded off for the crew accommodation.

The lower deck has 18 cabins (making 30 in all) of similar dimensions, the two after ones being the largest, 18 feet by 16 feet each, with stern windows. Before the lower deck cabins is a roomy space for troops. [*Illustrated London News*, 15 June 1844]

It is interesting to note the persistent preoccupation with the weight of her possible armament. This and the reference to troop-carrying are an indication that war was still very much a part of the business of expanding commerce. The *Monarch* had a working life of just over 30 years, going missing on a passage from Bombay to Rangoon in 1876.

Smith's response to the *Monarch* was made two years later when they launched the *Marlborough* (1,402 tons) on the Tyne, a ship which, put on to the Australian run in 1853, made the passage from the Lizard to Hobson's Bay in a mere 78 days. She and her sister ship the *Blenheim* 'were presented with silk ensigns and house-flags as being the finest ships in the British Merchant Marine'. That was at the Great Exhibition in 1851.

The *Marlborough*'s most famous passage was the return one in 1853 when she went from Port Phillip to the mouth of the Channel in 83½ days. Again the *Illustrated London News* provides a contemporary account:

The *Marlborough* (Allen W. Young, commander) weighed from the Port Phillip Head, on the evening of the 4th July, and passed out the same night through Bass's Strait to the westward, with a strong north-west gale, which increased until 6th July, at 4 p.m., when it blew a perfect hurricane, and the ship was in a most perilous position; whilst running with the wind quarterly, she broached to from a heavy sea striking her on the quarter, the main topsail blew to ribbons, and the ship was thrown almost upon her beam-ends; the lee side and lee quarter boat being buried in the water. The gusts of wind were also so terrific that it was impossible to stand against them, whilst the tops of the sea were blown completely over the ship. The barometer stood at 28·90 during the height of the gale. This happened in lat. 39° 55′ S., long. 142° 10′ E. off the south-west coast of Van Diemen's Land.

On the morning of 6th August in lat. 58° 50′ S., long. 80° 26′ W. a huge iceberg was seen ahead, the ship passing about a quarter of a mile to leeward. The thermometer fell to 29° Fahrenheit, when the *Marlborough* was close to the berg, and it was with difficulty that she steered clear of the large loose pieces of ice that were floating around the mass. The height is stated at about 525 feet; length half a mile, north side abrupt and bold; lee or south side, undulated surface and opaque, resembling frozen snow. The wind was blowing fresh from the N.N.W., and the sea was moderately rough. The sky was cloudy; and the temperature, when about two miles from the berg, not very cold, the thermometer being at 32°. The iceberg was visible from the deck of the ship about three hours. The *Marlborough* passed Cape Horn on the 8th August, and experienced strong gales until in lat. 35° south. She passed the tropic of Capricorn 30th August, and arrived in the Channel on the 26th September thus making the rapid passage from the southern tropic of 27 days; and 83½ to Start Point. . . .

A particularly interesting point about this passage is that the ship carried a Lascar crew and they were the first ever to go round the Horn.

But for all the free-thinking of the English builders and all the improvements they

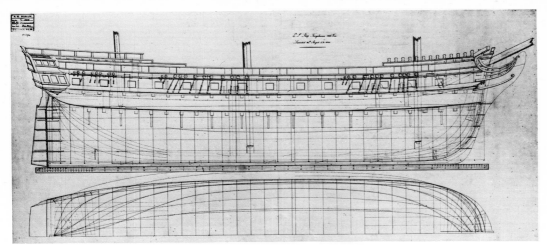

48   Lines of the East Indiaman *Farquharson* (1820), 1,326 tons

achieved in size and performance, they were still adapting and extending existing ideas; and in the end it was the Americans who initiated the fundamental changes in concept that finally revolutionised design and cleared the way for the sailing ship to reach the pinnacle of perfection as an artefact.

John Griffith of New York was the man responsible. His big idea came from the 18th century when, during the War of Independence, the Americans began building for speed instead of carrying capacity and produced the brigs and schooners known collectively as the *Baltimore Clippers*. Long, low, and flush-decked, they were designed to operate as privateers and slavers, but some of them finished up as plain pirates. Lubbock locates the yard where they originated very precisely as being in St Michael's, Talbot County, where 'the art of shipbuilding had been handed down from father to son for generations'; and he says the chief features of the Baltimore clipper were:

> . . . great beam, placed far forward, giving a very fine run from a high bow with plenty of sheer to a low stern. Both stem, sternpost and masts were unusually raked and it was this feature in the masts of a ship, together with a low freeboard, which, in the eyes of a stranger, gave immediate cause for anxiety and alarm, for any vessel described by the lookout as a 'rakish looking craft' was at once suspected of being an ocean free-lance.
>
> [*The China Clippers*, p 2]

Besides slaving and piracy, these small, fast craft, or others built on the same lines, were also engaged in the opium trade, particularly in the 20 years between 1830 and 1850. This traffic between India and China was illegal and those running it were smugglers. As such they 'showed greater daring and finer seamanship and made bigger profits than any the world had previously known' (ibid., p 3). Indeed, vast fortunes were accumulated in those two decades and it was the clippers that made the returns so fabulous by beating the monsoon and making the trade independent of it.

> These vessels had to make the passage round to China under racing canvas at all seasons and weathers, and especially during the strength of the N.E. monsoon, when they had to thrash their way to the Chinese Ladrones against a heavy head sea and strong current, either in the open or by the Palawan Passage.   [ibid.]

Thus was this unconventional type of ship tested and proved in action; and John Griffith decided the key to her wonderful performance was the shape of her bow. This

87

was his starting-point and in 1841 he delivered a series of lectures on the science of ship designing, in the course of which he made proposals about the lines and proportions of deep-water ships so radical that adopting them would constitute an absolute revolution in shipbuilding. But, though he backed his ideas with a model, they were greeted with scepticism and even ridicule. Nevertheless, he persisted and in 1843 the firm of Howland and Aspinwall gave him his chance. Working for them in the yard of Smith and Dimon, he designed and built the first of the great Yankee clippers.

She was the *Rainbow* (750 tons) and she cost $22,500 to build. The arguments about her went on all the time she was under construction and they grew considerably more vehement as her shape began to emerge. Hitherto, the full rounded bow had been one of the inescapable and immutable facts of life. It was this that gave lift and buoyancy to the fore-end of a ship and without it she would tend to bury herself even in good weather, while in bad she would ship so much green water that her decks would be untenable and she herself unmanageable. If this was true – and shipbuilders had believed it for a thousand years – then the *Rainbow* was a nightmare and shipping aboard her would be the same as committing suicide, for Griffith had 'turned the hull inside out', giving her concave bow lines that were against the laws of nature. That was the extreme view and even those who were prepared to admit she looked good could not believe it was possible to sail her.

> The chief innovation in her design was the sharpness of her ends. Instead of the full barrel-shaped bow, with cutwater and figurehead projecting beyond the stem in what was poetically termed in old naval architecture 'the sweep of the lion,' she had a long, sharp, knife-like entrance with concave water lines, which carried her greatest breadth of beam very much further aft than was usual; and the heavy quarters and lumping stern were lightened and relieved by rounding up the ends of the main transom. She had an unheard of amount of dead-rise, and was far more wall-sided than any vessel of her date. As to her proportions, she was given more beam to length than was considered safe by old salts. [ibid., p 24]

The *Rainbow* was launched in January 1845 and immediately went into the China tea trade. Presumably being such a revolutionary ship, there were things about her to be learned and adjustments to be made; but all this was done on her first voyage and on

49 Canton in 1847, showing old and new factories.

her second she showed her true worth. Leaving New York on 1 October 1845 she went out to Canton in 92 days and came home again in 88, making the round trip in a total of 6 months and 14 days. Her master, Captain John Land, was not only sure he had the fastest ship afloat under his command but convinced nothing could ever be built to beat her. Her life was short, for she disappeared on a passage from New York to Valparaiso in 1848 and is assumed to have foundered somewhere off the Horn; but 'she had done her work by starting a fleet of clipper ships which raised America to the level of Great Britain among maritime nations' (ibid., p 25).

Aspinwall's next ship was the *Sea Witch*. She carried the startling ideas of the *Rainbow* a little bit further and, in spite of Captain Land's prediction, matched, and on some passages even bettered, her performance. Her bow was longer and still more hollow than the *Rainbow*'s, and for figurehead she had an enormous Chinese dragon with a trailing tail that emphasised the length and fineness of her lines forward.

> *Sea Witch* had a sharp rise of floor (16 degrees it is said); she required a deal of ballast, indeed it is probable that she was somewhat overmasted, for she was noted for her heavy rolling and there was more than a whisper that she was unstable. [ibid., p 27]

Her first master was Robert H. Waterman, one of the most famous of hard-driving Yankee skippers, who was known as Bully Waterman. He personally supervised the rigging of the ship and obviously had fast passages in mind as he did so because when it came to sails she had everything – skysails, royal studding sails, square lower studding sails with swinging booms, ringtails, and every other flying kite known at the time. Her first voyage began on 23 December 1846 and she was back in New York on 25 July 1847, having taken 104 days out to Hong Kong and a mere 81 home from Canton. On her second trip she clipped another 3 days off the homeward passage, at one stage averaging 275 miles a day for eight consecutive days and making a best day's run of 289 miles. After a life of ten years she was lost on the coast of Cuba, coming home from Amoy with a cargo of coolies.

Generally speaking, developments in ship design have come in response to some specific and pressing demand on the resources of the carriers. For example, in the present decade super-tankers to haul oil from the Middle East to Europe round the Cape have come into being *since* the Suez Canal was closed to shipping. Deep down in the minds of the people involved in producing the clipper ship there was, no doubt, a recognition of the need to meet the challenge of steam; but as a motive it would be a great deal less obvious in the 1840s than it is today, and with the coming of the clipper in 1845 and the discovery of gold in California in 1848, it must have looked as if for once the means to see something done had arrived before the need to do it.

In a world where railways and telegraphy were still in their infancy and radio was yet undreamed of, the news of the gold find spread at a fantastic rate, the wonder of it increasing as it went. This El Dorado was no fable; it was a fact; and the lure of it pulled in great waves of people from every corner of the earth. It was providing transport for them that finally established the American Mercantile Marine as a force to be reckoned with in the carriers' world.

The Californian coast was remote, used only by hide-droghers like Dana's *Pilgrim*, and there was no easy way to it. The gold-seekers and those who opted for making a fortune out of supplying their needs, had three possible routes before them: overland across the United States; via the Isthmus of Panama; and round the Horn all the way by sea. The quickest was the mail route to Colón by steamer, then across the Isthmus on horseback, or by any other means offering, and up the Pacific coast by ship; the toughest, as well as the most risky, was by prairie schooner overland, with thirst and hostile Indians added to the normal hazards of long journeys; the slowest, and in the end the surest, was the long haul via Cape Horn; and the wise ones who had the choice made this their way. Consequently, the pressure on the carriers' existing resources during 1849 and 1850 was extreme. 'Every sort of vessel that would float was pressed into service, from the crack China clipper to the superannuated Indiaman, from the nimble New York pilot schooner to the war-worn veteran of the Nantucket whaling fleet . . .' (ibid., p 35). In those two years a total of 760 ships sailed round the Horn from American ports alone and they carried among them 27,367 passengers. It must be assumed that in addition to these there were a number of coffin-ships that sailed and were never heard of again; and among those that did make the Golden Gate many stayed put – for the crews, as badly bitten by the gold-bug as the passengers were, deserted on arrival and headed inland for the diggings. Lubbock quotes one ship – the *Niantic* – which was beached in what is now the centre of San Francisco and used as a doss-house. A door was cut in her side and over it was painted the legend: *Rest for the weary and storage for trunks.* Another, the *Apollo*, became a saloon and a third, the brig *Euphemia*, became the first prison in the booming city.

Suddenly ships had become as profitable as gold-mines and in spite of the hazards of the Cape Horn passage they were a very much surer way to fortune. Everybody who knew the difference between a bowline and a belaying pin, and a lot who had no clue about either, wanted to be in on it, and every tin-pot shipyard and weed-choked slipway along the New England coast began working round the clock. All sorts of people from farmers to house-carpenters now called themselves shipwrights and they did not have to live by tidewater to get into the racket. Some groups built their vessels in the woods, felling the trees on the spot for the purpose, then hauling the finished hull to river bank or sea-shore with teams of oxen and rollers; and the thought of driving that green timber south of the Horn and all the way up the Pacific coast must have been something of a nightmare to those in the know. But these were the speculators, after the fast buck and caring nothing at all about ships. One of those that did care was Sam Hall, and another was Donald Mackay of Boston who has been called 'one of the greatest shipbuilders that the world has known'.

Hall's most famous ship was the *Surprise* (1,361 tons). She was the first ever to be fully rigged on the stocks, being launched with her skysail yards across and her running gear already rove off. A particularly beautiful ship, she was remarkable for the fineness of her under-water body – Lubbock gives her 30 inches dead-rise at half-floor – and the height and spread of her sails. Her mainmast was 84 feet long and on it the mainyard 78 feet across. For her maiden voyage she loaded 1,800 tons of cargo in New York and, clearing for California, 'passed through the Golden Gate on the 96th day out'. This compares with the *Pilgrim*'s 150 days just 20 years before. From San Francisco the *Surprise* went on to Canton where she was chartered to load tea for the English market at £6 per ton. That voyage was so successful it earned her owners a clear profit of $50,000. After that she piled up a wonderful record of fast passages and finally 'struck a sunken rock beating into Yokohama and became a total loss' (quotes from Lubbock's *The China Clippers*, pp 39–40).

But the most famous of all American clippers was Mackay's *Flying Cloud* (1,793

50   American clipper *Surprise* (1850), 1,361 tons

tons). She was 208 feet long in the keel and 225 feet overall, with a beam of 41 feet and a depth of 21½ feet. With only 20 inches dead-rise at the half-floor, she was much fuller amidships than the *Surprise*. Her mainmast was 88 feet high and her mainyard 82 feet long. Sailing on 3 June 1851, she was a mere 89 days to San Francisco – in spite of a long spell of calms in the doldrums and the loss of main and mizen topgallant masts when only three days out. It was a fantastic performance of which Lubbock has recorded the details:

> *Flying Cloud*'s daily average was 222 statute miles, and her best run 374 knots in a corrected day of 24 hours 19 minutes 4 seconds. This worked into statute miles makes the 24 hour run as much as 427·5 miles. In all she sailed 17,597 statute miles at a rate of nearly 10 miles an hour.   [ibid., p 47]

From San Francisco she went on to China, doing another 374 miles in 24 hours first day out, proving the first one was not merely luck. She was in Honolulu in 12 days that time and back in New York 94 days after leaving Canton.

Her master was Captain Josiah Perkins Creesy, a wonderful seaman and one of the toughest that ever trod a poop-deck. He was famous for driving his ship to the limit and notorious for the brutal treatment he habitually handed out to his crews. A knuckle-duster came as familiarly to his hand as a sextant did and to him a belaying pin was as much a weapon as a piece of ship gear. He was always carrying away spars and just as frequently, or even more so, he had part of his crew in irons.

The *Flying Cloud* eventually came into British ownership and was on the Australian run for some years. But she finished up in the Canadian lumber trade and was burnt out in St John, New Brunswick, in 1873.

Like Boston, New York enjoyed its share of the boom in shipbuilding associated with the Californian gold-rush. As many as 10,000 men were employed in the East River yards and one firm alone – William A. Webb – built altogether 130 ships with a total tonnage of 177,872. Webb's *Challenge* (2,006 tons) was the biggest ship of the period. She was 230·6 feet long, 43·6 feet beam, and 27·6 feet deep. 'In design', says Lubbock, 'she was meant to go a step further than the sharpest clipper afloat, and she had no less than 42 inches of dead-rise at half-floor' (ibid., p 50). He goes on to quote a Captain Clarke:

> Her mainmast was 97 feet and mainyard 90 feet in length, and the lower studding sail booms were 60 feet long. With square yards and lower studding sails set the distance from boom end to boom end was 160 feet. She carried 12,780 running yards of cotton canvas, which was woven specially for her by the Colt Manufacturing Company. Her mainsail measured 80 feet on the head, 100 feet on the foot, with a drop of 47 feet 3 inches and 49 feet 6 inches on the leach.

Her first master was the infamous Bully Waterman whose brutality is supposed to have caused the death of a number of his foremast hands aboard her. One story is that he regularly stood behind the man at the wheel and clubbed him for any error he might make. 'One night he beat three men into unconsciousness, one after the other – the first for having dirty hands, and the other two for not understanding the compass' (ibid., p 55). Then, off the Horn, his mate acting on his instructions is reputed to have kicked three men, exhausted and half-frozen, off the mizen topsail yard into the sea. The mate himself finished the passage ironed hand and foot in the port quarter lifeboat where he was barely kept alive on bread and water. But Waterman overreached himself when he clubbed an old Italian seaman to death. When the ship reached San Francisco he had to hide from a mob of miners out to lynch him and eventually he was put on trial for the crime. He managed to buy himself out of trouble, but never went to sea again, mainly because nobody would sail under him. Curiously, he became religious in later life and did voluntary mission work about San Francisco Bay. But he could never live down his reputation and, on boarding one ship, he was recognised by some of her crew who had sailed with him.

> These men threw him overboard, and were busy trying to drown him by shoving him under the water with a long pole when the harbour police rescued him. He died on his farm (in Solano County, California) in 1884 at the age of seventy-six.   [ibid., p 59]

51   American clipper *Flying Cloud* (1851), 1,793 tons, which
eventually came into British ownership

The *Challenge*, under a new master and with a new crew, made a good run from San Francisco to Shanghai, but she failed to produce the great things expected of her. Her best day's run on her maiden voyage 'was 336 miles under all plain sail with wind abeam'.

So far the Americans were having it all their own way. There is no denying they had a positive genius for designing fast sailing ships and driving them to the limit, but there were other factors operating in their favour, notably the archaic English tonnage law, which taxed a ship on the basis of her length and beam but not her depth, and the Navigation Acts, aimed at cornering the English carrying trade for British bottoms. The first encouraged shipowners to go in for short, deep ships which were of necessity slow; and the second, by keeping out competition, made experiment and innovation unnecessary. Why bother when the Navigation Acts gave them their cargoes anyhow!

In 1849 the Navigation Acts were repealed and the Americans immediately began carrying tea for the London market. Their first tea clipper to run into the Thames was the *Oriental* (1,003 tons) and she had the whole of London staring at her in wonder.

Built by Jacob Bell of New York and launched in 1849, the *Oriental* was 185 feet long, 36 feet beam, 21 feet deep. On her first voyage she went out to Hong Kong in 109 days and back home to New York in 81. But it was on her second voyage that she made her name:

> On the passage out she left New York on 19th May, 1850; had very scant N.E. trades; crossed the Line in long. 30½° W., 25 days out; log to the Line 3,904; best day's run 264 miles. Took 45 days to Cape Meridian. Best run from the line to the Cape Meridian 300 under double reefs part of the time, the breeze N.W. fresh. From lat. 42° S., long. 31° E. to long. 97° E., she averaged 264 miles a day, best day 302, worst 228, for 10 days. Passed St. Paul's Island 58 days out. Reached Anjer 29th July, 71 days out, and arrived Hong Kong 8th August, 81 days out, averaging 200 miles a day.   [ibid., p 70]

She was immediately chartered by British shippers at £6 per ton of 40 cubic feet, although the current rate was only £3 10s. per ton of 50 cubic feet. She loaded 1,118 tons of tea and the freight on it paid the owners back almost three-quarters what she had cost them. On the homeward passage, she was 91 days to the Lizard and berthed in the West India Docks 6 days later.

With this voyage the American clipper tightened its grip on the China tea trade; but in spite of the general air of gloom and despondency in British shipping circles, there was still one growing point on the eastern side of the Atlantic Ocean and one man with a special kind of vision. He was Alexander Hall of Aberdeen. Out of his own head, ten years before the *Oriental* sailed triumphantly up the Channel, he had created an improved hull form. The modification was simple: '. . . it consisted in carrying out the stem to the cutwater and giving a ship a long sharp bow instead of the old-fashioned apple-cheeks' (ibid., p 71). The first ship he built was used on the run between Aberdeen and London, and immediately set a new record for fast passages.

In the next nine years he produced no fewer than 50 ships averaging around 600 tons each, and other builders began to base their designing on his model. Among these was one called Hood, working for the Aberdeen White Star Line, already a big name on the Australian and China runs. Then in 1851 Hall launched the *Chrysolite* (471 tons) and was ready to challenge American supremacy. The new ship was 102 days out to

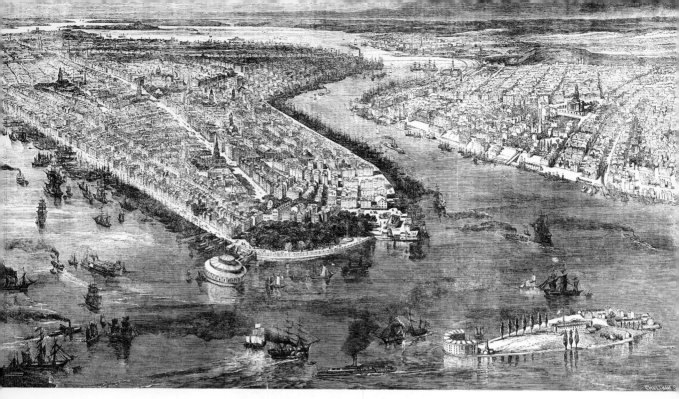

52　New York in 1855, the water front crowded with shipping

Hong Kong, though 'she had a very bad time running her easting down' (i.e. crossing the Indian Ocean from the Cape), the weather conditions being so extreme that she was frequently swept by seas breaking aboard over the stern. Even so, she knocked 19 days off the *Oriental*'s record of 89 to Anjer and she made the homeward passage from Whampoa in 103 days, in spite of losing all three topgallant masts in a heavy squall off the Azores. Running free under all sail 'she logged a steady $12\frac{1}{2}$ to $13\frac{1}{2}$ knots' and on that first voyage she covered '29,837 miles in 206 days'.

In 1852 the *Chrysolite* was first home with the new season's tea, a fact of such general importance and interest that it was noted in the current issue of the *Liverpool Mercury*:

> *Chrysolite* was docked on Saturday morning at 9 o'clock and before night a considerable portion of the cargo was landed, weighed, duty paid, and about 100 chests of tea were on their way to distant parts of the Kingdom, and a quantity of it was in the hands of retail dealers in the town, so that no doubt it was actually upon the tea tables of some of the people of Liverpool the same night – an instance of despatch unparallelled in this or any other port of the Kingdom.

The ship was 104 days out from Whampoa and the quotation shows the kind of pressure to which the seafarer as carrier was now being increasingly subjected. The leisurely, stately days of the Indiamen were indeed gone for ever!

American competition was undoubtedly a powerful stimulant to British ship-builders, but it was not the only one; for while the rush to the Californian diggings was still in full spate, gold was discovered in Australia. This was not so much gold in fine particles that had to be laboriously washed out of gravel and sand but nuggets that only

94

needed to be picked up – or so the stories went. Indeed, some of the hunks recorded were enormous – the *Welcome* nugget, found at Ballarat, weighed 183 lbs. and was valued then at £8,376; another, the *Blanch Barkley*, picked up in South Australia, scaled 146 lbs. So to lots of people it began to look as if the crock of gold at the foot of the rainbow was real and this was it, and in no time at all the English shipowners had a new emigration wave on their hands. The size of it can be gauged by the fact that in the next three years (1851–4) the population of Australia was trebled, which means upwards of 600,000 emigrants were shipped out there in the period; and in the next 30 years the number of people living in that remotest end of the earth had increased to over 2,300,000.

To meet the demand, ships were taken off the Indian run and sent out to Melbourne – the famous voyage of the *Marlborough*, noted earlier, being such a transfer. On that trip she took out 325 passengers and brought back only 60, making up her freight with '72,000 ounces of gold, valued at £288,000'. The demand also brought new names into the carrying trade – one of the most famous being George Marshall, the Sunderland shipbuilder whose *Statesman* (874 tons), built in 1849, now made the fabulously fast passage of 76 days from Plymouth to Melbourne.

In the ten years from 1851 to 1860 inclusive, 50 Blackwall frigates were built. They included such famous ships as T. and W. Smith's *Hotspur* (1,142 tons), Wigram's *Kent* (998 tons), and Duncan Dunbar's *Northfleet* (986 tons), which was run down off Dungeness by a steamer in 1873 with the loss of 293 lives, and his *Duncan Dunbar* (1,374 tons). Of these, probably the most widely known was the *Kent*. It might be said she was already out of date when she was built, yet she had a fantastic record and was considered to be one of the finest ships in the world. Lubbock describes her as:

> . . . 186 feet long with a beam of 33 feet. Her poop ran almost to the mainmast and she had a large topgallant foc's'le. She was, of course, full in the bow compared to the Liverpool clippers; she had the heavy square frigate stern with large stern windows and quarter galleries, and great heavy channels to drag through the water.

Her main royal masthead was 130 feet above her deck, which gave her a tall sail

53 A gold rush encampment in woods at Eaglehawk Gully, Bendigo, Australia

plan for her size and length and her bowsprit and jibboom were of unusual length, even for a Blackwall frigate. She came out with single topsails, with the usual four rows of reef points. Her yards were banded every 3 feet with iron, and strength was given to her for sail carrying by every device of the riggers' art then known.

[Lubbock, *The Blackwall Frigates*, p 152]

A cabin passage aboard her cost 80 guineas 'including wines, beer and spirits'; second cabin £35; and third cabin £25. Her average to Melbourne was around 80 days and her best, made in 1854, 78.

But the Blackwallers were the flower of an earlier age and the hopes of a future for sailing ships all lay with the clippers. Hall of Aberdeen began using iron for beams in them as early as 1852 when he launched the *Cairngorm* (938 tons). Finer in line and stronger than any British ship yet built, she was the first real challenge to the supremacy of the Americans. Her first run home with tea from Shanghai was made in 110 days. Then in 1853 Scott's of Greenock came into the business with a ship that was about ten years ahead of her time. She was the *Lord of the Isles* (770 tons), built entirely of iron and measuring 190 ft 9 in. × 27 ft 8 in. × 18 ft 5 in. Contemporary seamen called her the *diving bell* because of the lavish way she shipped water, and her master, a man called Maxton, '. . . used to say that she dived in at one side of a sea and out at the other'. But she was fast and drier inside than any wooden ship had ever been. On her maiden voyage she was only 70 days out to Sydney, and her record run home from Shanghai was 89 days in 1858. She was lost at sea by fire in 1862 on passage from Greenock to Hong Kong, the passengers and crew all getting clear of her before she went and making Macao in the boats.

A new triangular trade – first leg out to Australia with emigrants, second leg across to China, third leg home with tea – was now developing and clippers were being built for it in Greenock, Liverpool, and even alongside the frigates in the Wearside yards; and what was learned in these years enabled British designers to wrest the palm from the Americans in the 1860s.

54 Lines of the tea clipper *Lord of the Isles*

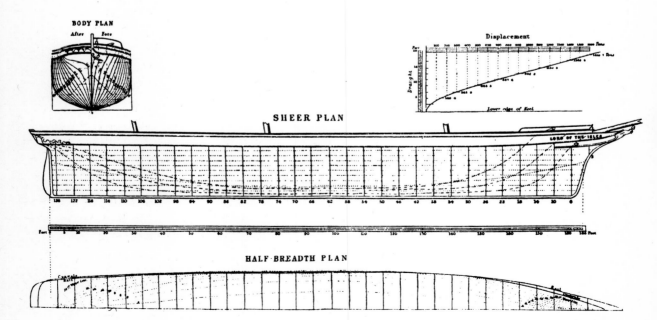

This was the decade in which the sailing ship reached the highest point in its development and the drive behind it was China tea – the annual race to get the first of the new season's crop into England ahead of everybody else. Lubbock lists 70 clippers built for the tea trade in this period. The names of many of them were still widely known at the turn of the century and a few remain famous even today – notably the *Sir Lancelot* and the *Cutty Sark*.

The first of these wonderful ships was the *Fiery Cross* (695 tons), built by Chaloner of Liverpool and launched in 1860. She measured 185 ft × 31·7 ft × 19·2 ft and there is a half model of her in the Science Museum at South Kensington. She was the first home in four seasons and only 24 hours behind the leader in another two.

In 1863 came the *Taeping* (767 tons; 183·7 ft × 31·1 ft × 19·9 ft) out of Steele's Yard in Greenock – whence two years later, and within a month of each other, also came the *Ariel* (852 tons; 197·4 ft × 33·9 ft × 21 ft) and the *Sir Lancelot* (886 tons; 197·6 ft × 33·7 ft × 21 ft). Lubbock quotes the following from a letter written by Captain Keay who commanded the *Ariel* throughout her career in the tea trade:

> Ariel was a perfect beauty to every nautical man who saw her; in symmetrical grace and proportion of hull, spars, sails, rigging and finish, she satisfied the eye and put all in love with her without exception. The curve of stem, figurehead and entrance, the easy sheer and graceful lines of the hull seemed grown and finished as life takes shape and beauty; the proportion and stand of her masts and yards were all perfect. On deck there was the same complete good taste; roomy flush decks with pure white bulwark panels, delicately bordered with green and minutely touched in the centre with azure and vermilion. She had no topgallant bulwarks (her main rail was only 3 feet high) but stanchions of polished teak, protected by brass tubing let in flush. . . . Ariel often went 11 and 12 knots sharp on a bowline, and in fair winds 14, 15 and 16 knots for hours together. The best day's work in south latitude, running east, was 340 nautical miles by observation, and that was done by carrying all plain sail except mizen royal, the wind being three or four points on the quarter. . . . [*The China Clippers*, pp 138–9]

The *Ariel* was a composite ship, which means she was constructed of wooden planking on iron beams and frames. The timber was teak down to the bilge with elm on the bottom. Her sister, the *Sir Lancelot*, was as like her as two ships could be, and she had for figurehead 'a knight in mail armour with plumed helmet, his vizor open and his right hand in the act of drawing his sword'. She spread 32,811 square feet of sail. The *Ariel* holds the all-time record for a sailing ship passage out to China made in the winter of 1866–7 when she ran from Gravesend to Hong Kong in 83 days, anchorage to anchorage, 79 days 21 hours from pilot to pilot; and in 1867 the *Sir Lancelot* came home in 99 days from Shanghai – the only ship to do the passage in less than 100 days that season.

The next great name is the *Thermopylae* (948 tons; 212 ft × 36 ft × 20·9 ft), built by Hood of Aberdeen. She was 'the pride of the British Merchant Service and justly considered by most seamen to have been the fastest sailing ship ever launched' (ibid., p 178). It was said she would do 7 knots with the wind so light that a lighted candle could be carried round the decks in it; yet she was a wonderful sea boat.

> With regard to her sail plan, she marked an advance in the direction of width of canvas as opposed to height. She had nothing above her royal yards, but these were tremendous spars. Her main royal was 19 feet deep and it required four men to put the gaskets on this sail. Her mainyard was 80 feet long, and her mainsail had a drop of 40 feet. [ibid., p 179]

97

55   The *Ariel* and *Taeping* racing up the English Channel in 1866

Her first voyage was an absolute triumph. Leaving Gravesend for Melbourne on 7 November 1868, she anchored in Port Phillip a mere 63 days later and from pilot to pilot her time was 3 days less than that. On that passage she made day's runs of over 300 miles nine times, the best of them being 330 miles. Loading at Newcastle, N.S.W., she went from there to Shanghai in 28 days, which was another record, then came home from Foochow with tea in 91 days, only the *Sir Lancelot* with 89 days bettering her time and nothing else within a week of it.

Then in 1869 came the most famous clipper of them all, the *Cutty Sark* (921 tons; 212·5 ft × 36 ft × 21 ft), built by Scott and Linton of Dumbarton for J. Willis. She was expressly designed to beat the *Thermopylae* and was the only ship ever to do so, except one that stole past her when she was slowed down with a foul bottom. Incidentally, the name 'Cutty Sark' comes from the poem *Tam o'Shanter* by Robert Burns and

> . . . Tam o'Shanter's beautiful witch, Nannie, with her long hair and cutty sark flowing in the wind, formed the figurehead of the new clipper and at the same time danced as a dog-vane at her main-truck. . . .   [ibid., p 188]

– a cutty sark being no more than a short shirt. As to speed, the new ship was known to do as much as 17½ knots and her best day's run was 363 knots, which is the most ever done by a *tea* clipper. The biggest-ever day's run for any sailing ship is claimed for the American-built *Champion of the Seas* (1,947 tons), which is reputed to have done 465 miles in one day running her easting down on passage from Liverpool to Melbourne in 1854. The *Cutty Sark*'s sail plan was reduced in 1880, 9½ feet being cut off her lower masts and 7 feet off her lower yards with other spars shortened to match. Nevertheless, she still logged 182 knots in 12 hours and ran from Sydney to the Lizard in 67 days, while

> . . . as late as 1892 she did a day's work of 353 knots when running the easting down and covered 2180 miles in the week. In 1890 she ran 3737 miles in 13 consecutive days

between the Cape of Good Hope and the Leeuwin. In 1889 she went from Green Cape to Sydney, a distance of 220 miles, in 17 hours and on another occasion sailed 7678 miles in 30 days.   [ibid., p 191]

While the tea clippers monopolised the headlines, men like Green and Wigram, and Smith continued to build frigates and to run them in the Indian and Australian passenger trades. Green built at Pile's Yard in Sunderland as well as at Blackwall, and about this time a new name appears among the carriers – the firm of Devitt and Moore. Altogether about 20 new Blackwallers were launched in the 1860s, among them the *Malabar* (1,219 tons), *True Briton* (1,046 tons), *Highflyer* (1,012 tons), and the *Parramatta* (1,521 tons). It is interesting to note how very little better in performance the clippers were when compared as a class with the frigates. Lubbock has produced a table in which he sets the passages to Melbourne made by frigate-built ships in 1860 alongside those made in the same year on the same run by Liverpool clippers. The 20 Blackwallers in his list include such flyers as the *Kent* and *Owen Glendower*, while among the same number of Liverpool packets he has the *Marco Polo* and the *Sovereign of the Seas*. The frigate *Suffolk* (957 tons) tied with the clipper *White Star* (2,339 tons) for the fastest passage, which was 70 days, and the average works out at 85 days for the frigates and 86 for the clippers. Why then, it may be asked, were clipper ships so inexorably superseding frigate-built ones? The answer lies in their comparative size and capacity. The biggest of those 20 Blackwallers was the *Monarch* (1,444 tons), the largest pay-load among them that of the *Kent* with 133 passengers; and they averaged 1,013 tons with 93 passengers and 57 crew. But the Liverpool ships averaged 1,525 tons, 270 passengers, and 53 crew. In other words, the clippers, earning more and costing less to run, showed a much higher profit and were a much better investment.

So far, all Green's Blackwallers had been wooden ships. The story is that Richard Green loved teak and oak so much that he could not bear the idea of iron in any of his craft. But he died in 1863 and his successors had no such prejudice. In 1866 they launched the first iron Blackwaller. She was the *Superb* (1,451 tons). A successful and popular ship right from her maiden voyage, she sailed for many years on the Australian run before being sold and she finished up under the Norwegian flag. Then in 1900, homeward bound with a cargo of manganese ore, she was dismasted and abandoned in the North Atlantic. Eventually plucked into Gibraltar, she ended her days there as a coal hulk.

The last of all the Blackwallers was also an iron ship, launched in 1875 as the *Melbourne* and later renamed the *Macquarie*. Built at the Blackwall Yard, she was 1,857 tons register and 269·8 feet long, and on her maiden voyage went out to Sydney in 84 days; but she made her reputation on her second voyage, going from her departure off Start Point to Sydney in 77 days. This passage was described in the *Nautical Magazine* as follows:

The *Melbourne* left the East India Dock on 10th June 1876 and Gravesend on 12th June, the pilot leaving her off Start at 6 p.m. on 15th June and a departure from the land being taken on the following day. Ordinary winds and weather prevailed to the tropics, which were entered on 2nd July, and after a tedious drag through the N.E. trades, which were exceedingly light, the Equator was crossed at midnight on 14th July in Long. 30° 30′ W. The tropics were quitted on 24th July, and so little easting was there in the S.E. trades, that the ship had to tack three times before clearing the South American coast.

99

The meridian of Cape Agulhas was crossed on 10th August, and after that the ship had it all her own way, strong fair winds prevailing. In running down the easting she sailed 5129 miles in 17 consecutive days or an average of about 300 miles a day, the best runs being 374, 365 and 352 miles a day. Cape Otway light was sighted at 3 a.m. on Thursday, 31st August, and the Heads were entered at 11.30 a.m., and but for the bad northerly wind which headed her coming up the bay she would have reached the anchorage on the evening of the same day. . . .

The *Melbourne* cost a mere £42,000 to build and equip 'ready for sea', and, after a working life of just under 40 years, she continued to serve the carrying trade as a store hulk at moorings in an Australian port.

But long before her keel was laid the wind of change was blowing strongly through the world of the carrier. This particular gale, like so much else that has profoundly influenced the life of the seafarer, was centred in the eastern Mediterranean where all this time the Frenchman, de Lesseps, had been shifting Egyptian sand. His great ditch, linking the Mediterranean with the Red Sea, was completed 13 years after he began digging. In 1869 it was opened to traffic as the Suez Canal and that was the end of the seafarer's Golden Age.

56   The *Melbourne*, renamed *Macquarie*, 1,857 tons, launched in 1875; 'perhaps the best known of all the Blackwall frigates' in her time. Her name was changed in 1888, when she was about to sail on her second voyage to Sydney

The Triumph of Technology

. . . the steamship began to work revolutionary changes in the nature and
geographical distribution of world trade. . . .

[Condliffe, op. cit., p 293]

THERE WAS NOTHING VERY TECHNICAL about the Suez Canal; no locks or lock-gates, no elaborate pumping machinery, and, over most of its length, no ballasting to its banks. It was indeed a ditch and recognisable as such in spite of its length and depth. The construction of it was essentially a pick and shovel job, involving a mere 200 million francs in capital, but 13 long years of toil and sweat and an untold amount of blood and tears. Evidence has been found showing that a similar waterway probably existed across the Isthmus in the time of King Seti I (c. 1380 BC), but that did not make the modern concept appear any less crazy in the first half of the 19th century to hard-headed people with their feet on earth and money to invest. Napoleon – a notorious dreamer of dreams – wanted to attempt it in 1798, but the experts persuaded him it was impossible because the waters of the Red Sea were 33 feet higher than those of the Mediterranean. In the end, however, the passionate conviction and single-minded persistence of de Lesseps broke down the opposition and it was done.

The Isthmus is flat and mainly featureless desert, but a number of small lakes are strung across it and the French engineer had the clever idea of using these to reduce the total length that had to be dug. Beginning at Port Said, the Canal runs along the edge of Lake Manzala, through the Bala Lakes, and then in turn through Lake Timsa, the Great Bitter Lake, and the Little Bitter Lake to Port Ibrahim. It has a total length of 103 miles, of which no less than 21 miles runs through lakes.

Financially, the Canal was an enormous success. Shares in it acquired by the British government in 1875 for £4 million were valued in 1945 at £32 million and in between they had paid close on £40 million in dividends. In 1880 it was used by 2,026 ships with a total tonnage of 3 million; by 1948 that number had increased to 8,686 ships totalling 55 million tons and in 1955 it reached 14,666 ships and 115 million tons – which breaks down to something like 45 ships for every day of the year. The effect of it on the carrying trade was dramatic in the extreme, but, to understand the more important developments to which it gave or helped to give rise, it is necessary first to look at the world of ships and shipping as it was in the periods immediately preceding and immediately after it was opened.

Throughout the third quarter of the 19th century the transport of migrating people continued to be a prime concern of the carriers, but by no means the only one, for after arriving at their destination – be it Canada, Australia, New Zealand, South Africa, or the U.S.A. – these thronging, thrusting people had to be serviced, their needs supplied, and the products of their labour taken to market. Doing this made ever-increasing demands on existing shipping and brought about great changes in the nature of the cargoes it carried as well as the routes it followed. Morton notes that

. . . up to about 1850 exports were mainly of articles for consumption, and above all, of

57 The opening of the Suez Canal in 1869 by Eugénie, Empress
of the French

cotton textiles. From that date larger and larger quantities of iron ware, rails, locomotives
and trucks and of machinery of all kinds were sent abroad.   [op. cit., p 389]

and there were other things besides machinery. It had been the custom for the tea
clippers to load outward with Manchester goods, making up the deadweight with lead
bars; and, while waiting on the China coast for the new season's tea to be got ready for
shipping, they would run cargoes of rice coastwise from Saigon and Bangkok to Hong
Kong and even as far as Japan. But in 1860 the *Flying Spur* (735 tons) went out with
general cargo to Sydney, loaded coal there with horses in the 'tween decks for Shanghai,
then tea home. This is one example of the new pattern for clippers and by this time the
Blackwallers were also diversifying. The *Sutlej* (1,150 tons) was destroyed by fire in 1859
while loading saltpetre and jute in Calcutta for England; in 1862 the *Kent* (959 tons)
left Melbourne with 250 passengers and a full cargo that included a large consignment
of wheat, another of copper ore, some casks of sperm oil, and £400,000 in gold ingots;
and in 1864 the *Lincolnshire* (1,025 tons) sailed from the same port with

> 2,000 bales of wool, 125 casks of tallow, 115 cases of whisky, 30 tons of case goods,
> 9,800 ounces of gold dust and 130 passengers. [Lubbock, *The Blackwall Frigates*, p. 218]

At this time world trade was completely dominated by Great Britain. A. J. Brown
in his *Introduction to World Economy* says:

> Britain in 1851 was the source of between a quarter and a third of all the goods which
> were sent out across international frontiers – a fact which becomes the more impressive
> when we realise that, since trade is essentially an exchange, no one country can normally
> be responsible for more than half of the world export total.   [p 145]

And the same authority underlines the quotation from Morton given above:

> Britain's exports in the 1850's were mainly the results of her industrial revolution; they
> were nearly all finished manufactures, two thirds of them being either textiles or wrought
> iron products. . . . In exchange for them the United Kingdom got mainly raw materials,
> especially the materials for its textile industries.   [ibid.]

Meanwhile, on short hauls and wherever reasonably cheap coal was available, the steamship was consolidating and advancing. Cunard made ever-more sure of the cream of the Atlantic trade by building bigger and faster steamers – the *Bothnia* and *Scythia*, both 4,500 tons, in the 1870s and the *Servia*, half as big again as that, in 1881. In the Mediterranean basin steamship-owners had virtually taken over the fruit trade of the Levant and were also running wheat from the Russian steppes out through the Bosphorus. Bunkering stations were established on the African coast and in the Atlantic islands, and in 1857 a monthly mail service to South Africa was started by the Union Steamship Company. The first vessel employed on the new run was the *Dane* (530 tons), a barque-rigged steamer which was under contract to complete the voyage in not more than 42 days. In 1863 the time was cut to 38 days and in 1876, when the service became weekly, it was reduced again, this time to 26 days. Everywhere, in fact, even before the Suez Canal was opened, the sailing ship was being challenged by steamship-owners muscling in on the most remunerative trade routes and taking the best of the cargoes. On passages to such places as India, China, and Australia the clipper and the Black-waller still held their own and, carrying top-grade cargoes at high freight rates, continued to prosper. With skilful masters taking advantage of the trade winds and the more or less constant westerlies in the high latitudes south of Agulhas, they could still show the best of the steamers the way and make the long haul in a shorter time. But elsewhere the writing on the wall was inescapably clear; and to sailing-ship men who looked ahead in those days, it must have seemed that the gods, jealous maybe of the almost perfect loveliness the clipper-builders had created, were out to destroy them – for the Canal was not the only thing working against them. There was also the American Civil War which broke out in 1861 and had been over something like four years when the Canal was opened.

The American Civil War, says Morton,

> . . . was at bottom a war to determine whether the future development of the U.S.A. was to be into an industrial country or one with a plantation economy, an economy in which foodstuffs and raw materials were produced for export by slave labour and which was governed by a slave-owning aristocracy. [op. cit., p 402]

But although it was an internal conflict and fought – apart from some relatively minor naval actions – exclusively on American soil, the effect of the Civil War on the

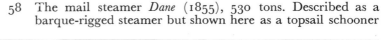

58 The mail steamer *Dane* (1855), 530 tons. Described as a barque-rigged steamer but shown here as a topsail schooner

Lancashire cotton industry was catastrophic – the recoil from it shaking the shipping world to its foundations and, in the end, considerably altering its shape.

Cotton had long been a basic element in the transatlantic carrying trade, for cotton was still the most important British industry, and in the main the raw material to feed it came from the United States. Thus in 1860 out of the 1,319 million lbs. of cotton spun in Lancashire, 1,115 million lbs. was imported from America and a mere 204 million lbs. from India – carted, of course, round the Cape. When the war erupted the American Federal forces immediately clapped a tight blockade on all the ports in the Southern States and that vast flow of American cotton was cut off at its source.

With their mills idle for want of raw material and 60 per cent of their work-force unemployed, the millowners made frantic efforts to whip up new supplies, and fresh cotton-fields were established in Egypt and India to fill the gap. By 1865 cotton imports from India had indeed risen to 446 million lbs., but it still had to come round the Cape, which made it much more expensive to use and cut deeply into the profit margins of the industry. So the opening of the Suez Canal four years later came to harassed millowners and workless cotton operatives, as well as shipowners with steamers laid up on their hands, like a gift from heaven.

The Canal cut the time for a passage to the Far East by weeks. One line of steamers began making runs to and from China in 42 days as against the 100 days plus of the fastest clippers. And, what was perhaps more important in the end, their voyages were scheduled to a degree impossible with sailing ships which could easily take a month longer over the same passage in successive seasons. The *Cutty Sark*, for example, did the run home from Woosung in as little as 108 days and yet on one occasion took 127 for it. The saving in the Indian trade was even more exciting – Liverpool to Bombay in

MAP NO. 11   The Suez Canal, showing how de Lesseps linked up
the lakes of the Isthmus

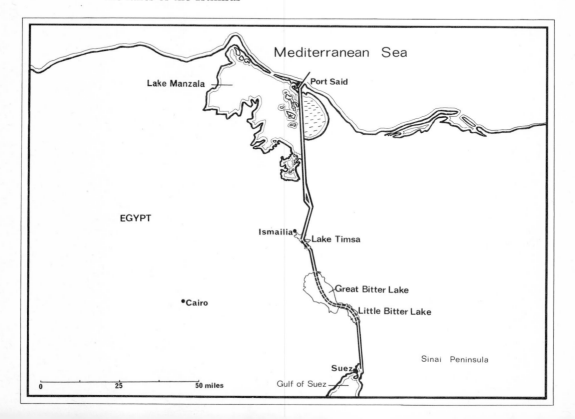

59 American Civil War. First battle of Bull Run, 21 July 1861. The Confederate army overruns the Federal guns, while other Federal infantry units flee over Stoe Bridge

30 days; how Vasco da Gama would have marvelled at it!

The immediate result of all this was a big drop in freight rates. Nevertheless, the 1870s saw a great boom in steamships and the yards building them were inundated with orders. One firm had six building at once on the Clyde in 1878 and offered to sell sixty-fourth shares in them for £560 a time – which makes their capital value something in the region of £36,000 each, compared with the contract price of £16,150 for the *Cutty Sark*. These new steamers were described as being 305 feet long, 34.5 feet beam, and 24.25 feet in depth, and their deadweight capacity was given as 'upwards of 2,900 tons'. It was claimed that this was the most profitable size for the Indian trade and that such a ship cost very little more to run than one of only 2,000 tons deadweight. The new ships were powered with surface-condensing, compound engines of 280 horse-power, designed to give them an average speed under working conditions and fully loaded of $9\frac{1}{2}$ knots, with a coal consumption of 16 tons in a 24-hour day. The boilers were large for the time and had a working pressure of 80 lbs. Cargo was the prime consideration and, in order that the maximum capacity should be available for it, the accommodation for 36 first-class passengers was in a deckhouse 'fitted with every requi-site to ensure their comfort in tropical as well as in cold climates'. Officers and crew were also berthed on deck. The vessels were to '. . . be worked on the most economical principles, not being hampered with extravagant salaries or expensive officials'.

With these six ships Messrs Cayzer, Irvine & Co. founded the famous Clan Line. They were built of iron and the first of them, the *Clan Alpine* (2,100 tons register), was launched by Stephens of Glasgow. She was brig-rigged and carried quite an impressive array of canvas. A sailing card dated 1879 advertises another, the *Clan Stuart* (2,200 tons gross register), due to sail from Liverpool to Bombay on 26 April that year and accepting cargo at 'through rates' for 'Coast Ports, Kurrachee and the Persian Gulf'. She carried a surgeon and a stewardess and the first-class passage in her to Bombay could be had for 35 guineas. The *Clan Stuart* finished up running pilgrims from India to Mecca and was finally scrapped in 1906. Of the other five, three made quiet ends, but the *Clan*

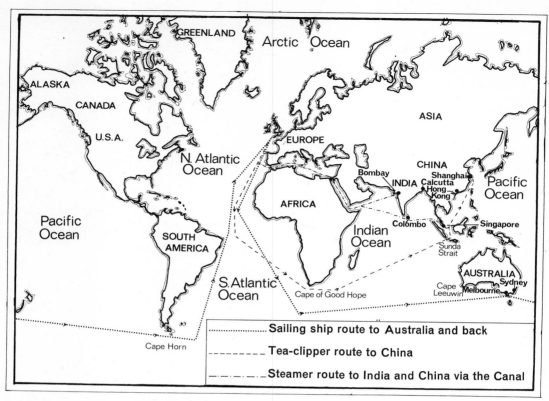

MAP NO. 12   Main trade routes after 1869

Lamont was lost off Ceylon in 1891 and the *Clan Gordon* off Durban in 1897.

The running expenses of these ships are of particular interest. For a voyage from Liverpool to Bombay and back in 1878, they were as follows:

Wages	£817	Insurance on Hull and Freight	£768
Provisions	565	Advertising, and Agents'	
Fuel	1,110	Commissions	465
Marine and Engine Stores	750	Incidental Expenses	30
Stevedores' and Port Charges,		Management and Office Expenses	232
Liverpool and Bombay	1,045		
Canal dues and Expenses			£7,482
Port Said	1,700		

Thus the use of the Canal on a single voyage cost half as much again as the bunkers out and home, or twice as much as the wages of the crew; but even so, it paid and the new companies flourished. The Glen Line was another one established to take advantage of the Canal. They made a bid for the tea trade and it was one of their ships, the *Glenartney*, that made the run home from Woosung in 42 days mentioned earlier. They have been a famous name on the short route to China ever since.

From this time on the carrying trade expanded at an ever-increasing rate, while the kind of things carried continued to change. Taking the growth element in British exports first, Condliffe notes:

Their average annual value in 1870–74 was more than fifteen times as great as in 1770.

[op. cit., p 287]

and throughout the next four decades British ships 'carried more than half the seaborne trade of the world', while British shipyards built two-thirds of all the new ships launched.

The effect of the Canal on the China tea and Indian cotton trades was immediately recognisable, but there were other less obvious ways in which it acted as a catalyst and opened up new possibilities. It allowed bunkering stations to be established in the mouth of the Red Sea and thus further strengthened the grip of the steamship on the carrying trade, but, above all, by reducing freight charges, it made it possible to haul basic commodities like wheat to markets half-way round the world from the point of production. This was supremely important in northern Europe and especially in Great Britain, where industrialisation had drawn so many people away from the land and agriculture into the factories. The result had been a big decline in home food production which, coupled with the natural increase in population, created an ever-growing demand for imported foodstuffs. This, like every other human need, threw up problems and solving them greatly accelerated man's progress towards the mastery of his environment. So

> . . . by the early seventies . . . railroads in various parts of the world had begun effectively to open up inland continental areas of rich fertility. The first trans-continental line in the U.S. for example, was completed in 1869. A gathering flood of cheap grain began to pour into the markets of industrialised western Europe, not only from the Middle Western plains of the U.S. but from Australia, India, Canada, Argentina, Russia and the Danube valley. . . .   [ibid., pp 288–9]

Grain was only the beginning. Experiments in refrigeration had been going on throughout the century – the first patent for a practical machine being taken out in 1834. Then in 1869 the first true refrigerated ship went into service. The new idea suffered from teething troubles, of course, but they were overcome, and Condliffe notes:

> In the late seventies meat began to be carried from the U.S. in refrigerated ships. It was not long before Canada, Argentina, Australia, and New Zealand were sending increasing quantities of chilled and frozen meat to Britain. Butter and cheese followed meat. . . .
> [ibid.]

And foodstuffs were not the only products of the 'newly opened areas' developed to satisfy markets overseas. Wool, for instance, was shipped in ever-increasing quantities from Australia, New Zealand, South Africa, and the Argentine. Then there was jute from India and other vegetable fibres, such as kapok from the East Indies, and vegetable oils from East Africa and other tropical regions. On this point Condliffe says:

> The opening of the tropics to cultivation for industrial markets was almost as important as the opening up of the last remaining temperate plains. Vegetable oils, lumber, dye-stuffs, spices and cane sugar were important items in this trade. . . . Moreover, the ever-growing consumption of minerals led to a search for new sources of supply. Gold was found in South Africa, Western Australia and Alaska; nickel in Canada, copper in Rhodesia and the Belgian Congo. Petroleum was sought all over the world.   [ibid.]

And everywhere production expanded at a fantastic rate in order to keep up with accelerating industrialisation and population growth.

> Ivar Hogbom has calculated for the period 1880–1913 the rates at which the basic minerals were produced. The regularity and rapidity of the increase are best revealed in his calculation of the periods during which production doubled. For petroleum the

60 The American
Shenandoah (see p. 120),
3,154 tons, was built
in 1890, capable of carrying
huge shipments of goods

doubling period was 8·6 years, for copper 13·1 years, for pig-iron 15·6 years, for phosphates about 16·5 years, for coal and zinc 16·7 years, for lead 19·7 years and for tin 20·1 years. . . . Such a geometric increase means that in each period, the amount produced equals the whole earlier world production. [ibid., p 298]

The change in character was equally comprehensive and dramatic. Until well into the 17th century the spice trade was the most lucrative business in which anyone could engage and huge fortunes were made out of it; but the 18th century saw a shift to sugar and tobacco – both produced by slave labour; then in the 19th century the introduction of Free Trade, followed by the final effective abolition of slavery and the opening of the Suez Canal, brought the final shift to 'cheap, bulky articles such as iron ore, coal, foodstuffs and fibres'.

As a result, in the fifty years preceding the first World War, the everyday life of the ordinary man changed more than in many preceding centuries. . . . Goods and services that had formerly been luxuries of the rich – white bread, meat, sugar, tropical cereals and fruits, tea, cocoa and coffee, leather shoes, new textile fabrics and patterns . . . became cheap, conventional necessities. . . . [ibid., p 294]

and the spread of knowledge was enormously extended by cheap newspapers and books 'printed on paper produced from remote forests'. Even the natural rhythm of seed-time and harvest was by-passed, for, with the whole wide world to draw from, commodities ceased to be seasonal. The arrival of wheat cargoes in the Port of London in 1905 shows to what extent this trend had developed by the end of the century:

In January cargoes arrived from the Pacific Coast of America, in February and March from Argentina, in April from Australia, in May, June and July from India. By July and August the winter wheat from the United States was coming in, and in September the spring wheat arrived, to be reinforced in October by Russian shipments. In November the Canadian wheat arrived. . . . [Professor Lilian Knowles, quoted ibid., p 296]

All this was a tremendous challenge to the carriers. It was also a golden opportunity which they seized with both hands and the increase in the amount of available shipping kept pace with the expansion in trade. Taking the Clan Line, mentioned

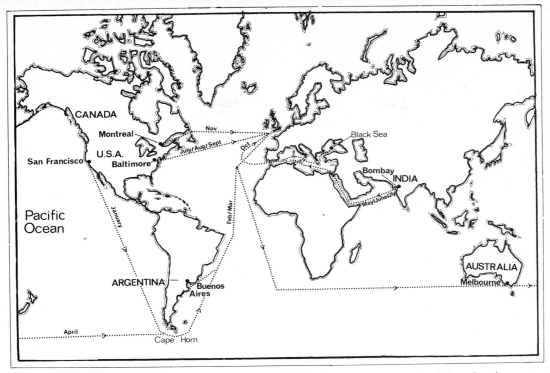

MAP NO. 13   Routes by which wheat cargoes reached London in 1905

earlier, as typical of a shipping company primarily interested in the transport of cargo and only incidentally concerned in the passenger trades, their inaugural clutch of 6 vessels had grown to a fleet of 27 by 1883, i.e. in a mere five years. They were building of steel now rather than iron and many of their ships, like the *Clan Matheson*, were around 4,000 tons register. A further flurry of building in the 1890s produced 28 new vessels for them in nine years and in 1900 the fleet numbered no less than 47 steamers.

A curious development in the nineties was the turret ship, a vessel with a revolutionary hull form designed and patented by William Doxford and Sons, the Sunderland builders. The story goes that she was conceived to beat the system of calculating dues for ships passing through the Suez Canal, but there is no hard evidence of this and other notable advantages over the orthodox hull form were claimed for her. The prototype was called the *Turret*. She had

> . . . a straight stem, with an entrance claiming to reduce the resistance to head seas; above the water-line the side-frames were turned, and after being carried partially across the harbour deck as beams, then swept up to the turret deck. There was no sheer on either deck. All the erections and hatches were on the turret deck, whilst the harbour deck was quite clear of fittings with the exception of small coaling ports and a light protection rail.
>
> [*The Clansman*, Autumn 1955, p 29]

The propelling machinery was aft in the original design but subsequently it was placed amidships, immediately abaft the navigating bridge.

In its final form the turret ship was supposed to have the following advantages:

1. A high navigating platform on which all vulnerable openings were placed.
2. The turret was an excellent feeder for bulk cargoes and the curved gunwale made for efficient stowage at the most dangerous point. No shifting boards or wooden feeders were needed.

3. Great strength with a smaller steel weight than usual.
4. Low initial cost.
5. Water could not lodge on deck in a position where it might tend to capsize the vessel.
6. Low tonnage, combined with a good capacity/deadweight ratio.   [ibid., p 30]

The most obvious disadvantages were the limited deck-space provided for working cargo and the difficulty of launching lifeboats from them in emergencies. After two had capsized at sea, the turret ships acquired a reputation for being *tender*, but whether this was justified or not is still a matter of controversy. The second item above would seem to refute the charge because the shape of the hull precluded the possibility of a bulk cargo like grain or coal shifting dangerously in a seaway. Even if it was not particularly well stowed and began to move in under the curved gunwale, the trunk would act as a feeder and the material standing in it would settle and prevent any large-scale movement developing. Indeed, this is the idea behind shifting boards (which are temporary fore and aft bulkheads) and wooden feeders or very deep hatch-coamings. For those who had to sail in them, the turret ships were tough going. The accommodation they provided for both officers and crew was cramped and uncomfortable, and when they were deep-loaded the seas running along the harbour deck took all the lift out of them, leaving an impression of sodden lifelessness most unpleasant to live with. In the end, however, the most curious thing about them was the abruptness with which building was stopped. Three different reasons have been advanced for builders abandoning the design: (*a*) that they were really dangerously unstable; (*b*) that alterations in the laws relating to tonnage dues wiped out their main advantage; and (*c*) that a more efficient and satisfactory type of vessel – the shelter-deck steamer – crowded them out. Whatever the explanation, after building 30 in the 11 years up to 1907, the Clan Line ordered no more and the turret ship gradually disappeared from the seafarer's world.

The last quarter of the 19th century, like any other period of expansion, was prolific in new developments and not all of them were so misconceived and short-lived as the turret ship. The one that affected the seafarer most profoundly was the rapid growth in the commercial use of petroleum.

61 The turret ship fully developed. S.S. *Clan Macfarlane*,
4,823 tons

There are several theories about the origin of petroleum, but the most widely accepted one is that it results from the decomposition of the remains of extinct marine organisms. It lies in pockets in certain rock formations and there are various places about the world where it seeps to the surface. Men have been using petroleum collected from these seepage areas since ancient times and some people believe the fiery furnace into which Shadrach, Meshach, and Abednego were thrown was such a seepage accidentally ignited; but the first true oil-well dates from no further back than 1859 when Edwin Drake began drilling in Pennsylvania and struck oil at a mere 69 feet. From that time on, the carriers had another commodity with which to cope and this one was not only difficult to handle but also dangerous.

Drake's initial production was only a few barrels a day, but the industry spread and though the U.S.A. is still the largest producer, many other countries are now involved in petroleum, among them Venezuela, the U.S.S.R., Kuwait, Saudi Arabia, Iraq, Libya, Canada, Iran, Mexico, and Indonesia. By 1955 the world was producing 795 million tons in a year and the drillers were going down to 20,000 feet to find new sources of supply. Petroleum products, whether in the form of aviation spirit, petrol for motor-cars, kerosene, diesel fuel, lubricating oil, or crude straight out of the ground, are generally referred to simply as *oil* and the ships that carry them as *tankers*. There are three ways of shifting oil in quantity from the point of production to the consumer – by pipe-line such as those across the desert from Iraq to the eastern shore of the Mediterranean; cased in drums, cans, or barrels which are then loaded into railway trucks, lorries, or ships; and in bulk in ships or tank-cars. From the very beginning it was recognised that whatever the distance, transporting it in bulk was the cheapest way. As a result, less than four years after the first well gushed, the ship-designers were at work on the problem of carrying oil in bulk by sea, and in 1863 sailing ships were being fitted on the Tyne with specially constructed tanks for the purpose. It could not have been highly thought of as a cargo because it was not until 1872 that Palmers of Jarrow built the first steamship expressly designed to carry it. She was the *Vaderland* and like the *Zoroaster*, produced in Sweden five years later, the tanks were built into her holds and were quite separate from her hull. Experiments were subsequently made in which the hull itself formed the tank and in 1886 the Tyne builders launched the *Gluckauf* (2,300 tons gross) which is reckoned to be the prototype of the modern tanker with her machinery aft and her hull divided into a number of separate tanks by transverse and longitudinal bulkheads.

The next important development came in 1908 when the method of construction was changed by introducing longitudinal framing instead of the conventional transverse system. This gave a stronger and at the same time a lighter hull, but there were snags and modern builders use a combination of the two.

In the early days oil was still rather a poor relation so far as the carrier was concerned, and it was not until the development of the internal combustion engine and the enormous extension of its use in automobiles that the tanker came into its own. Then, some time between the two World Wars, some far-sighted expert realised that not only was shipping in bulk the cheapest way of transporting oil, but also that the bigger the bulk, the cheaper it would come – or, to put it another way, a given quantity of oil could be shifted more cheaply in one big ship than in two small ones. After that everybody in the tanker-building business began thinking on a big scale. First came the 10,000-tonners, then the giants of 15,000. Many people thought that was pretty near

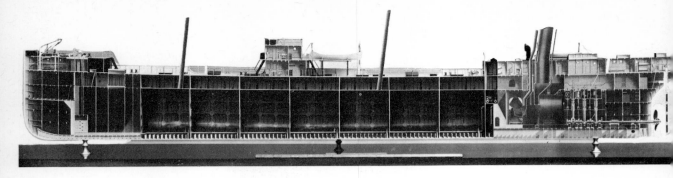

62   Sectional model of early tanker (1891). Note triple
expansion engines immediately abaft boilers and funnel

the limit, for the old problems of stability and longitudinal strength were nagging again;
but in the 1930s the 20,000-ton mark was passed, and when war broke out in 1939, the
biggest tanker afloat was the *C. O. Stillman* (24,000 tons deadweight). The war held
things up for a while, but as soon as it was over the yards were building tankers of
28,000 tons deadweight which were followed almost as soon as they took the water by
32,000-tonners. In 1953 the *Tina Onassis* (45,230 tons deadweight) started hauling oil
out of the Persian Gulf and she was the first of several. These were the biggest ships the
Suez Canal could take, and for a while it looked as if they would be the biggest ever
built for the trade; but in 1956 political trouble in the Middle East induced second
thoughts and it was realised that shipping oil round the Cape instead of through the
Canal could be a profitable undertaking provided the tankers used for it were big
enough. As a result of this new thinking, the *Universe Leader* (85,505 tons deadweight)
came out that same year. She was built to run between the Persian Gulf and the
Atlantic coast of America, and after she had proved herself the sky was the limit.
Tankers of 100,000 tons came next and very soon even they had ceased to evoke any
wonder, being succeeded by 150,000-tonners and bigger. The following report, from
a newspaper of 30 October 1968, brings the story up to date. It is date-lined *Bantry*,
Ireland:

> The world's biggest ship sidled into the bay here today so slowly and cautiously that she
> seemed nervous of knocking the Emerald Isle down. *Universe Ireland*, first of six identical
> mammoth oil tankers built in Japan, had arrived with 312,000 tons of crude oil from
> Kuwait to open a man made oil well for Britain and Europe in this remote corner of
> Ireland, a favourite spot for summer tourists. *Universe Ireland* is not a thing of beauty. She
> is blunt and broad beamed. Fully laden she squats low in the water with 80 feet of the
> hull beneath the water-line – like some monstrous black iceberg. She inched into Bantry
> Bay at no more than three knots, shepherded by four powerful tugs specially built to cope
> with the complex docking procedures for a ship 1,135 feet long. . . . It takes two miles to
> bring the *Universe Ireland* to an emergency stop . . . she is tall as a 10 storey building. . . .
> [*Sun*, 30 October 1968]

American owned, the vessel flies the Liberian flag and carries a fantastically small crew
of 52 hands, mostly Japanese from the island of Okinawa. Her sister ship, *Universe
Kuwait*, was due in the same port only two days later. Bantry Bay is the only place in
Europe capable of handling ships of this size and the terminal there was specially built
for them at a cost of £10 million.

As noted above, petroleum production with a doubling period of 8·6 years is by

112

a long way the fastest growing enterprise in which man is currently engaged, and the following table, based on *Lloyd's Register* statistics, shows how the world's tanker shipping has grown to keep pace with it. The figures are in millions of tons gross:

Year	All Shipping	Tanker Shipping	% Tanker	
1930	68·0	7·6	11·2	
1939	68·5	11·6	16·9	
1948	80·3	15·6	19·4	
1956	105·2	28·2	26·8	[*Everyman's Encyclopedia*]

Tankers were developed for a specific purpose – the transport of petroleum products in bulk – and they are good for nothing much else unless it is carrying water to arid areas in time of drought; but the backbone or broad base of the carrying trade in the period of expansion after the opening of the Suez Canal was the 9-knot *three-legged* tramp-steamer which was good for anything and could and would go anywhere to do it. She was called *three-legged* because of her power unit – the triple expansion, reciprocating steam-engine which had three of almost everything, cylinders, pistons, connecting rods, crank-throws, and sets of valve gear. It has been said that the supremacy of the British in the carrying trade round the turn of the century was based on the triple expansion engine and the Scottish engineers who built and ran them. In 1893 Kipling celebrated both of them in his *McAndrew's Hymn* and the following year he did the same for the ships with *The Mary Gloster*:

> They piddled and piffled with iron, I'd given
>   my orders for steel!
> Steel and the first expansions. It paid, I tell
>   you, it paid,
> When we came with our nine-knot freighters and
>   collared the long-run trade!

The great virtue of the engine was its fantastic reliability. There is no poetic licence whatsoever about Kipling's description of McAndrew's particular set 'slam-banging

63   The tanker
     Universe Ireland

113

home again . . . after ninety days o' race an' rack an' strain. . . .' They would stand any amount of abuse and keep running long after a more sophisticated piece of machinery had packed up and fallen to pieces.

The next development in marine engines was the introduction of the turbine, pioneered by the Tyneside firm of Parsons. In 1897 they built the *Turbinia* expressly to demonstrate their marine steam-turbine to the Admiralty. The vessel, which was nothing more than a vehicle for the engine, reached the then fabulous speed of 34·5 knots and thereafter, although the triple expansion reciprocating engine continued to be widely used, the turbine was established for use in naval ships and the more luxurious forms of passenger transport. Its advantages were light weight and small size plus a smoother motion than could ever be achieved by the reciprocating engine. It was particularly suitable for large passenger ships because it required less headroom and could be accommodated on a single deck. The first merchant ships to be powered by turbines were the Allan Liners *Victorian* and *Virginian* and the Cunarder *Carmania*, all launched in 1905. The *Carmania*, rated at 21,000 horse-power, was so successful that the Company's next two ships, the *Lusitania* and *Mauretania*, built in 1907, were given turbines and knocked up a speed of 26 knots in service. The *Mauretania* subsequently held the blue riband for the fastest Atlantic crossing for 22 years and once averaged 25·5 knots for 27 consecutive voyages. Not even the triple expansion reciprocating engine could beat that for reliability, but the running costs would be a different matter. Nevertheless, 30 years later when the first of the great Queen liners – *Queen Mary* (80,000 tons) – came into service in 1936, she had turbines as propelling machinery. The decision to install them rather than any other type of engine was made by a committee of experts whose brief was to equip her for a speed of 28·5 knots, which was estimated to require a shaft horse-power of 158,000. They gave her:

> . . . twenty-four water-tube boilers for the propelling machinery and four Parsons turbine units each consisting of one high-pressure, one intermediate-pressure, one second inter-mediate-pressure, and one low-pressure turbine for ahead propulsion, each driving a separate pinion engaging with the main gear wheel. For astern propulsion a high-pressure impulse stage is incorporated in the second intermediary. A separate turbo-generator supplied electric power for deck machinery, auxiliaries, lighting and hotel service. Three cylindrical boilers supplied steam for heating. The daily fuel consumption is 1000 tons.
>
> [*Everyman's Encyclopedia*]

64   The original turbines used in
     T.S. *Turbinia* (1894)

65   Turbines for T.S. *Queen Mary* (1934)
     under construction at Clydebank

With the internal combustion engine developing so rapidly and oil supplies expanding as they were, the introduction of the motor-ship was the next logical step. Denmark was the first in the field with the *Selandia*, launched in 1912. She was a twin-screw ocean-going vessel equipped with Burmeister and Wain four-stroke engines developing a total of 2,400 horse-power. The advantages of the motor-ship over other types are formidable. First and most obvious, they need no boilers, feed-pumps, feed-heaters, or filters, so their propelling machinery occupies less space and requires a smaller crew to run it; then they can be bunkered much more rapidly and cleanly and their fuel can be stowed in the double-bottom, leaving more space available for pay-load; and finally they have what the experts call 'higher thermal efficiency', which results in lower fuel consumption, cheaper running costs, greater range of operation between stops for refuelling, and considerable saving in both time and money. In spite of the great benefits accruing from its use at sea, however, the internal combustion or, as it is more generally known, the diesel engine took longer than the steam-turbine to win over the carriers. In 1914 the whole world could boast of a mere 297 motor-ships with a total tonnage of 234,247 gross. In 1919 there were still only 912 ships adding up to 752,606 tons gross; but the turning-point came in the 1920s and by 1931 the figures had risen to 4,080 and 9,431,433 respectively. The increase continued and in 1956 no fewer than 15,554 out of all the ships afloat were driven by diesels. They had a total tonnage of 37,503,741 gross, which was roughly 35 per cent of the world's gross tonnage at that time.

That 1956 world total of 105·2 million tons gross included a wide variety of ships, but they were all mechanically propelled and, so far as the carriers were concerned, sailing ships were long since extinct. The moment of truth for them undoubtedly came on that day in 1869 when the first steamer passed from the Mediterranean into the Red Sea via the Canal; but of course they did not disappear overnight. There was too much history wrapped up in them for that, too many people still believed in them and, perhaps more important, too much money was invested in building and running them. Those already in service continued to run and what happened to one flyer was in essence the fate of them all. They were squeezed out. Only the details in the doing of it were different from ship to ship.

Taking the *Cutty Sark* as an example, she was launched a week after the opening of the Suez Canal, so in a way she came into existence in a world that had already outgrown her; and when she sailed on her maiden voyage on 16 February 1870 she had already achieved notoriety by bankrupting her builders. At that time under all plain sail she spread 32,000 square feet of canvas. This is no less than three-quarters of an acre and it is estimated that the power developed by it was equal to that of a 3,000 horse-power engine. (Taking a motor-ship at random for comparison, the Standard Oil tanker *Narragansett*, built in 1936 to do 16 knots loaded, developed only 600 horse-power more. Her tonnage was 10,389 gross and the *Cutty Sark*'s only 963.) The famous windjammer's owner was John Willis, a one-time master in sail whose father, another of the same breed, was reputed to be the Old Stormy immortalised in the shanty *Stormalong*. It was his ambition to win the race home with the new season's tea from China, but in spite of her fantastic sailing qualities, the *Cutty Sark* never did it. Always the luck seemed to be against her. She failed in the beginning because her first master, though extremely competent, was no *driver* and lost his chances through over-caution. On another occasion, she left Woosung in company with the *Thermopylae*. They passed

Anjer and came into the Indian Ocean with only a mile and a half between them and then the *Cutty Sark* began to pull away. Twenty-six days later she was 400 miles ahead; but at that point she lost her rudder in a heavy gale and by the time a jury one had been made and hung off, the race was over for her. (Losing rudders was quite a habit with her. The second one went in a West Indian hurricane in 1909 and the third in 1915 when she was four days out from Lisbon on a passage to Mossamedes under the Portuguese flag.) In 1873 under a new master, again competent but cautious, she made her first voyage to Sydney with general cargo. The owners still had hopes for her in the tea trade and from there sent her to Shanghai with a load of coal. After discharging she went to Hankow, 600 miles up the Yangtse and towing all the way, to compete with the steamers for a cargo of tea. She got it and took 118 days on the passage home. After that the competition grew fiercer year by year, until, in 1878, she was squeezed out altogether and lay in Shanghai unable to get a cargo. Her master died there, presumably still hoping, and she was taken over by her mate who was the kind of *driver* she had lacked since her first sailing. He took her to Sydney in ballast, returned to China for the next tea season, again failed to get a cargo, and returning to Melbourne loaded wool for New York. Nobody knew it at the time, but that was the start of the slide for her.

Outward bound in 1880, she had trouble with her foremast hands and the mate struck one of them so hard he was dead when he hit the deck. The master locked up the mate, but put in to Anjer and let him slip ashore there under cover of darkness. This caused more trouble with the crew and, four days after leaving the port of call, the master himself went out of his mind, jumped overboard from the taffrail, and was never seen again. This left the second mate in command and he took her back to Anjer, narrowly missing leaving her bones on Thwart-the-Way Island as he went. A Dutch pilot then took her to Singapore where another master was appointed. He was

> . . . incompetent as a seaman, fat in person, hypocritical, a bully and a physical coward; a man who affected to be deeply religious, but whose only real devotion was to the bottle.
> [Frank G. G. Carr, *The Cutty Sark*]

Under this character she carried the first cargo of Indian tea ever shipped to Australia, took a cargo of coal to China, and went in ballast to Cebu to load jute for New York. There both master and mate were investigated by the British Consul who suspended their certificates. The man sent out to take over the command found the ship in a shockingly neglected condition and her gear practically unworkable. After getting her back into proper shape, he brought her home to London where her spars were cut down, and in 1883 she was committed to the Australian wool trade. Her crew of 28 was now cut to a maximum of 22 and sometimes she sailed with as few as 19; and now for the first time she really fulfilled herself, making runs like 79 days from the Channel to Newcastle, N.S.W., and 82 days home. This is a curious comment on the unpredictability of sailing-ship performance. The *Cutty Sark* was designed for the China tea trade which, being a fine-weather run, demanded that a ship be fast in light winds. She was not built for Cape Horn weather or the wild westerlies of the South Pacific between Australia and Tierra del Fuego; but she revelled in them, and now beat the best.

In 1885 she was taken over by her most famous commander, Captain Richard Woodget, and it seemed as if he was the man she had been waiting for. Frank G. G. Carr says of him:

> Never was a more fortunate appointment made to the command of any ship. Woodget, the son of a Norfolk farmer, had gone to sea the hard way, as a hand in the East coast

66 *Elbe Ore*, a modern bulk carrier

billyboys and coasters. In that hard school he had learned his seamanship, as the great Francis Drake had done before him; and he had learned, too, how to get the best out of a ship, in all weathers. [ibid., p 16]

Woodget was then 49 and in his prime as a seaman. He was a real *driver* and right from the beginning showed what he could do with the ship:

Leaving the East India Dock on 1st April, 1885, she was only 20 days out when she crossed the Line; and passed the meridian of the Cape 26 days later. She then sailed 931 miles on a wind in 70 hours; and on 4th June, still close-hauled, made a day's run of 330 miles in 24 hours. Her time for the whole passage out was 77 days from the Start to Port Jackson, Sydney; and this, a day better than the next ship, the *Samuel Plimsoll*, made her the winner of the race out. [ibid., p 18]

The passage home was also outstanding. She was in the Channel only 67 days out from Sydney, beating the *Thermopylae* by 12 whole days; then she lost the wind and took 5 days to cover the next 305 miles. Even so, she was in the Downs in 73 days, which was a week better than the *Thermopylae*.

Bad luck caught up with her again in 1886, although some people might prefer to call it bad management. Tea was still the great lure for the owners and, loading her with the only cargo available, which was scrap iron, they sent her out to Shanghai. Arrived there, she waited three and a half months for a cargo, but the tea trade was now so firmly in the hands of the steamship companies that the shippers were not interested in her and in the end she went on to Sydney in ballast. She was now too late for that wool season and had to lay up to wait for the next, but when she got it, hers was again the fastest passage home – 72 days this time against the *Thermopylae*'s 87.

There were no more gambles with tea and the ship, still under Woodget, continued to make record passages both out and home in the wool trade until 1894, when she left Brisbane with 5,304 bales of wool, which was a record quantity for her. She was so deep with it that her Plimsoll mark was 2 inches below the water when she sailed. The passage took her 84 days to the Start and when he brought her into London, Woodget was told by the owners they were selling her to the Portuguese.

117

This was too much for Captain Woodget and though he was given another ship – the *Coldinghame* – he made only one voyage in her, then left the sea and bought a farm in his native Norfolk, where he lived out his days and died in 1928 at the age of 82.

The ship, now 27 years old, was re-registered in Lisbon as the *Ferreira* and for the next 26 years she ran as such under the Portuguese flag. She was employed in various trades, the most definite of them from Lisbon to Rio de Janeiro, then to New Orleans and back to the Tagus, a trip she made annually for several years. In 1922 she was beginning to show the effects of her 54 years of battering about the seas of the world; but in the autumn of that year Captain Wilfred Dowman of Trevissome in Cornwall bought her back, had her towed home to Falmouth, and set about restoring her to her former glory. She lies now in a specially constructed dry-dock at Greenwich, the last survivor of the Golden Age.

For the builders and designers of sailing ships the story was much the same – no sudden collapse, but a steady squeeze against which they fought a battle that was long drawn out and sometimes profitable, but for them always bitter because they were on the loser's end. The following figures from *Lloyd's Register* and the Board of Trade returns are quoted by Lubbock in *The Last of the Windjammers*:

> In 1860 there were 25,663 sailing ships afloat with a net tonnage of 4,204,360 tons against 2,000 steamers with a tonnage of 454,327 tons. In 1868 sail tonnage reached its high water mark with 4,691,820 tons, steam having risen in the meantime to 824,614 tons. Then came the Suez Canal, and by 1873, by which time its value was fully realised, the tonnage of sail had dropped to 4,067,564 whilst that of steam had risen by leaps and bounds to 1,680,953. Then sail, helped by the rapid increase of the wool trade from the colonies, the jute trade from Calcutta and the grain trade from San Francisco, made a great effort and for a few years its tonnage rose again. The next spurt came between 1889 and 1893, when there was a short boom in big steel four-posters. [vol I, p 116]

The statistics of building as distinct from the Register itself are even more illuminating:

> In 1860, 818 sailing ships were built, of which 786 were either wood or composite whilst only 32 were of iron. The steam total was only 198, of which 149 were of iron. Five years later the sailing ship total had risen to 922 ships, registering 249,400 tons, only 116 out of this total being of iron. In 1870 only 541 sail were built, 63 of which had iron hulls. The small increase in 1875, when 566 sail were built, 193 of which were fine iron ships, again drops back in 1880 to 316 ships, all except 39 of which were small wooden craft. By this time steamships had passed the sailing ships' total with 408 ships built and a tonnage of 485,661 tons as against sail's 59,845. [ibid.]

The iron clipper reached its peak in 1873 and 1874 when Potter of Liverpool, Harland and Wolff, Stephens of Dundee, and others were building 1,700-tonners for such firms as Brocklebank, Corry, and Carmichael's Golden Fleece Line. This increase in size seemed to offer the only hope of countering the competition of the steamers, and to cope with the larger hull some revolutionary change in rig was necessary. It came in 1875 with the *Tweedsdale* (1,403 tons), a barque with four masts instead of three. She was the first of what seafarers have always called the *four-posters*.

In 1880 there was still good money to be made owning sailing ships, for there were three big trades into which steamers had not then penetrated. They were the jute and rice trade, based on Calcutta, Chittagong, and Rangoon; the Pacific grain trade out of San Francisco and Puget Sound; and the Australian wool trade. There were also plenty of cargoes to be had on the west coast of South America, though these, being mainly nitrates and guano, were still considered a long way beneath the dignity of top-class ships and those who ran them. Outward cargoes from England were still largely made up of Manchester cotton goods, heavy machinery, steel rails, coal, and salt, and a sign of the times for those who could read portents was the growing number of first-class sailing ships in the Welsh and north-east coast coal ports. With the tea and passenger traffic and everything else that demanded quick scheduled transit lost to the steamship, speed was no longer the primary consideration in sailing-ship design and from now on the clipper shape was abandoned for a bigger, full-bottomed hull designed expressly for the greatest possible carrying capacity.

The years 1880–4 were a boom period in shipbuilding and, with steel replacing iron as a basic material, the price of new ships fell steadily until, in the late summer of 1884, as little as £14 a ton for a first-class sailing ship and £10 15s. a ton for a third-class one was being quoted on the Clyde. This compares with the £21 a ton paid for the *Cutty Sark* 15 years before. The boom was wonderful while it lasted. It produced ships like the *Garfield* (2,290 tons) and the *British Isles* (2,394 tons). But the inevitable slump consequent on over-production followed and that winter 54 big deep-water sailing ships were waiting for grain cargoes in San Francisco Bay. Some of them had been there for months, and other outports as far afield as Calcutta and Melbourne were equally congested.

It was about this time that some of the biggest and oldest firms in the business began to think of withdrawing. To do so must have been a difficult decision to take. Rankin, Gilmour & Co. of Liverpool had reached it before the boom began. The *British Isles* was Beazely's last ship; the *Holkar* (3,073 tons), a four-masted barque said to be the largest sailing ship in the world when she was built in 1888, the last of Brocklebank's; and the *California* (3,099 tons), launched in 1890, the White Star's final venture in sail. A curious exception to the general trend was the Shire Line of Thomas Law. They grew instead of contracting and, starting in 1870 with only two 700-ton ships, reached the turn of the century with a fleet of 24 sailing ships averaging 1,558 tons each.

67 The French *France II*, 5,633 tons, launched in 1911, the largest sailing ship ever built

The Shire Line was built up in the Australian emigrant trade. But even they built their last sailing ship in 1896. She was the *Duns Law* (1,640 tons), a ship subsequently destroyed by fire in 1904 while in harbour at Iquique.

All this time the Americans were also building big, but still in wood. Starting with the year the Canal was opened their high points were:

1869	*Glory of the Seas* (2,130 tons)	1890	*Shenandoah* (3,154 tons)
1873	*Three Brothers* (2,972 tons)	1892	*Roanoke* (3,347 tons)
1889	*Rappahannock* (3,054 tons)	1902	*Atlas* (3,381 tons)

These were wonderful ships. The *Rappahannock* cost $125,000 to build and her hull alone contained 1,200,000 feet of pine and 706 tons of Virginia oak. For her maiden voyage she went from Philadelphia to Japan with case oil, which is another name for petroleum in cans. Her cargo was 200,000 gallons and she sailed with a deck crew of only 20 men. She had a short life, going from Japan to San Francisco for a cargo of grain which she discharged in Liverpool. She then left England with a cargo of soft coal for San Francisco, but the coal fired by spontaneous combustion just after she got round the Horn and she never made it. Instead she was burnt to the water's edge in Cumberland Bay on the island of Juan Fernandez, but the crew got ashore safely and were ultimately rescued. The *Shenandoah* was a four-masted barque and Lubbock says she cost $175,000 to build. She

> . . . spread no less than two acres of canvas. Her fore, main, and mizen lower masts were built spars of Oregon pine measuring 38 inches in diameter, and 90 feet in length from deck to cap. Her top masts were 56 feet long and topgallant masts 68 . . . her fore, main and mizen trucks were 217 feet above the deck . . . and her mainyard was 94 feet long.
> [Lubbock, *The Down Easters*, p 174]

The *Shenandoah* loaded the biggest cargo of grain ever taken out of San Francisco by a sailing ship. It totalled 5,300 tons and was valued at $175,000. The great ship remained in service until 1910, when she was sold for $36,000 and cut down into a coal barge.

To some degree American sailing-ship owners were better placed geographically than the British to meet the challenge of the Suez Canal and the 9-knot, three-legged tramp-steamer; but the pressure was on them too, and in the end they were forced back into what was essentially a local pattern of voyaging with three focal points – the Alaska salmon fisheries, the Hawaiian sugar trade, and the west-coast coal and lumber trades.

In the 1890s practically all deep-water sailing-ship passages were made one way or the other round Cape Horn, and the sea in its vicinity was often crowded with windjammers of all nationalities. The master of the barque *St Mary's Bay* had between 30 and 40 ships in sight when off the Horn in 1895; but this was in a period of minor boom with cargoes to be had for the asking. It did not last and by the end of the century the sight of a big sailing ship in ballast was becoming more and more common as it became more and more difficult for them to get a charter. They ranged far and wide in search of a cargo – London to Cape Town and even London to Melbourne according to Lubbock. In the end even this failed them: they began to lay up for months on end in obscure creeks about the world. From time to time efforts were made to get them going again, Eriksson of Mariehamn with his Australian wheat fleet being one of them; but even this came to an end between the wars and then only a handful of square-riggers remained, carefully preserved, heavily subsidised, and run as training ships by maritime-minded governments. Such in the beginning was the famous German four-masted barque *Herzogin*

Cecilie (3,242 tons gross), built at Bremerhaven in 1901, the French *Richelieu* (3,100 tons), and the Danish five-masted barque *Kobenhavn* (3,965 tons gross), which Lubbock claims to be the largest sailing ship ever built in the British Isles. The *Kobenhavn* might be ruled out by the purist because, having a diesel engine capable of driving her at 6 knots, she was really a compromise with technology.

There is no end to the wonder of sailing ships. A simple list of famous windjammers and the records they achieved would by itself make a sizeable volume and three items that could well find a place in it are:

1. The last square-rigger to sail under the British flag was the *Garthpool* (2,842 tons), originally built for the Calcutta jute trade as the *Juteopolis*.
2. The largest sailing ship ever built was the five-masted barque *France II* (5,633 tons), launched at Bordeaux in 1911.
3. The longest passage of a sailing ship was made by the *Garthwray* (1,891 tons). She took 559 days from Grangemouth to Iquique with a cargo of briquettes in 1922–3.

As might be imagined, this savage competition between the sailing ship and the steamer bore as heavily on the seafarer as it did on his ships. For him the Golden Age was finished even before the Suez Canal was opened. In terms of money and social prestige the decline began with the advent of steam and the exit of the Honourable John Company, and by the middle of the century the master had lost a great deal of his autonomy. He was no longer answerable only to Almighty God and his own conscience, but had to satisfy a manager and board of directors and obey their behests; while for remuneration, he was receiving something like £20 a month if he was lucky. Of course, being the sort of man he was, he made it up a bit on the side and Lubbock quotes the master of the iron clipper *Nelson* (1,248 tons) as an example. Around 1864 the ship was in the Indian trade and at Bombay the master

> ... had already made a good profit on 100 tons of provisions, rope, etc., for which he had paid freight space; in addition to this he had filled the spare cabins with 500 of the best York hams, which cost him 1s. per lb. delivered on board and sold in Bombay at 1 rupee 4 annas per lb. or 2s. 5d. in English money. He also landed 196 out of 200 cases of sulphuric acid. These, being dangerously inflammable, had been stored on deck and four had been broken in rough weather off the Cape – for each case landed he received a perquisite of 20s. On the homeward run he paid freight on 30 large cases of coffee on his own account. . . .   [*The Last of the Windjammers*, vol 1, p 127]

It is estimated that he cleared £1,000 on this voyage over and above his wages. But such opportunities did not come every trip nor to everybody and, besides, that kind of juggling was ultimately debasing. In the long run it must have affected not only the public image of the shipmaster but his private one too. The next inevitable step was cutting down on the provision bills and taking a *come-back* from the ship-chandler. Organisation is tighter and there is less scope for swindling today, but between the wars there were shipmasters who had earned the label *belly-robber* and their names stank accordingly.

That salary of £20 a month in 1864 was down to £186 a year when Richard Woodget took over the *Cutty Sark* in 1884, which was a miserable pittance for a man with his qualities and the kind of responsibility he carried. He would have been better off in a steamer where the master's rate was £20 a month for the first two years and £25 thereafter. But even this had been reduced by 1893 to £18 a month on joining and £1 a month extra for each year of service up to a maximum of £25. Many did go into steam,

68 Samuel Plimsoll
(1824–98). A
portrait in oils by
R. H. Campbell

but the lucky ones got out of ships altogether before age and their misspent youth caught up with them. It saddens one to remember the others – and they were plenty.

Materially, however, there have been gains as well as losses for the seafarer in the technological age, and the possibilities of exploiting the foremast hand have been progressively reduced by legislation. Now he is protected in regard to wages, accommodation, food, discipline, hours of work, life-saving apparatus, and the general equipment and maintenance of the ship in so far as it bears on his safety and comfort. Moreover, while his way of life remains high on the scale of hazardous occupations, it is less uncertain and onerous because of such inventions as radio telegraphy and telephony, the gyroscopic compass, echo-sounder, and radar.

Perhaps the most important law ever enacted for the protection of seamen was the section of the Merchant Shipping Act of 1876 which instituted a maximum load line. This is more generally known as the *Plimsoll Line* after the Bristolian of that name who forced the idea on to the Statute Book. The law is quite specific about it. A *Load Line Certificate* is issued only after a surveyor has satisfied himself 'that the vessel is structurally efficient and is provided with the necessary effective protective protection for ship and crew'. Four authorities are empowered to assign load lines to British ships. They are the Board of Trade (B.T.), *Lloyd's Register of Shipping* (L.R.), the British Corporation Register of Shipping and Aircraft (B.C.), and the British Committee of the Bureau Veritas (B.V.).

The load line is now a conspicuous feature on the sides of every ship and not only its position but also its size and shape are carefully prescribed. Thus it must include:

The *deck-line*, which shall be a horizontal line 12 inches in length and 1 inch in breadth, marked amidships with its upper edge passing through the point where a line continued from the upper surface of the deck intersects the outer surface of the shell plating.

The *load line disc*, 12 inches in diameter, intersected by a horizontal line 18 inches in length and 1 inch in breadth, the upper edge of which passes through the centre of the disc. The disc shall be marked amidships below the deck line.

Horizontal lines, 9 inches in length and 1 inch in breadth, which extend from and are perpendicular to a vertical line marked 21 inches forward of the centre of the disc, and which indicate the maximum depth to which the ship may be loaded in different seasons and circumstances. These lines are as follows:

The *Summer Load Line* shown by the upper edge of the line passing through the centre of the disc and also by the upper edge of the line marked S.

The *Winter Load Line*, shown by the upper edge of the line marked W.

The *Winter North Atlantic Load Line*, shown by the upper edge of the line marked WNA.

The *Tropical Load Line*, shown by the upper edge of the line marked T.

The *Fresh-water Load Line, in Summer*, shown by the upper edge of the line marked F.

The *Tropical Fresh-water Load Line*, shown by the upper edge of the line marked TF.

Statutory Freeboard is the distance between the Statutory Deck Line and the respective load lines, actual freeboard is the distance from the Waterline to the deck line.

[*Reed's Seamanship*, p 415]

The load line legislation was welcomed by all who merely worked ships about the world; but those who made money out of running them saw it as a dangerous threat to the liberty of the individual in general and their own profit margins in particular. Consequently they exerted great pressure on successive governments to have the law amended, and in 1906 the load line was raised to meet their demand. Again in 1929 amendments were made to permit deeper loading in the case of tankers and ships carrying deck cargoes of timber. At this time overloading was still a fairly common practice among tramp-steamers, particularly on long passages between less highly developed countries in which officials could be *sweetened* to turn a blind eye; but with the very much greater degree of detailed organisation that exists in shipping today there is no profit in it any more and any master who tried it would soon be out of work.

So there has been a slow but progressive levelling up in the last hundred years, and materially the foremast hand is better off today than he has ever been; he has less discomfort to endure and virtually no hardship at all to suffer, while the hazards he has to face are fewer and very much less terrifying; his pay is better and secure, his hours are shorter and regulated by law; and, finally, he is no longer casually employed but belongs to a pool of labour which makes sure he has a reasonable time ashore between voyages and pays him for it.

69   The *Encounter Bay*, a container ship loading in Rotterdam

Masters and officers are similarly safeguarded but something has gone from them with their autonomy. They no longer stand out among people. In a crowded subway the man in a bowler-hat carrying a furled umbrella could just as well be a shipmaster as a bank manager, the one in the black jacket and pin-striped trousers, a second mate as a lawyer's clerk.

As for the ships, they are still changing to meet changing demands. Just as the steamer skimmed off the cream of the passenger trade in the second half of the 19th century so the aeroplane is monopolising it today. Taking the North Atlantic crossing as an example:

> In 1954, the ships carried nearly a million passengers and the airlines under 600,000. In 1964 the airlines carried 3,500,000 passengers, while the ships' traffic had sunk to just over 700,000.   [*The Times*, 12 July 1965]

In the same issue *The Times* shipping correspondent declared: '. . . . passenger ships on the Atlantic are no longer really necessary. People who have to get to the other side can fly there; and most of them do'. This trend will continue and with the development of bigger aircraft it will accelerate. Consequently a new pattern is already emerging. The two super-liners, *Queen Mary* and *Queen Elizabeth*, following the example of Brunel's *Great Eastern*, are ending their days at moorings as super-fun-fairs; and the *Queen Elizabeth II*, completed in 1968 at the cost of £29 million, can never break even as a legitimate passenger ship. She is to be a part-time carrier and hopes to fill in with holiday cruises. In other words, she has been built for prestige and the entertainments industry rather than the carrying trade.

Elsewhere *specialisation* is the great thing – special ships for special trades; refrigerated tankers for liquid gas; ships that are designed for heavy mineral ore, for paper, for timber, for big lifts like locomotives and power-station plant; and *container* ships for general cargo for which '. . . cargo is prepacked in big containers and loaded and discharged in hours rather than days'.

And the keyword now is *organisation*. Everything down to the last rivet and final lick of paint, the percentage of bone and fat in the crew's beef, even the time it takes to peel a bucket of potatoes, must be worked out beforehand on the basis of cost-effectiveness or some other accountants' catch-phrase; every unit of equipment and consumption from a breakfast egg or a drum of white lead to a spare piston or tail-end shaft, begins as an entry on a printed form. Thereafter, it moves from form to form and is never lost sight of for a moment until it is consumed, and even then the record of it remains for reference. Moreover, mechanisation is everywhere and year after year the demands made by the carrying trade on the wit and ingenuity, as well as the nerve and fortitude, of those most directly involved in it, become less and less. This is progress and all to the good of the great majority; but attached to it, as to every other step forward made by man, there is a price-tag. Kipling tried to decipher the figures on it when he wrote his *Song of the Dead*; but that was in 1893 when the actualities of today were still mere trends and portents, and it is obvious now that blood was only part of the price of progress – a down payment or deposit. The balance has been called in since. As well as the wild beauty that took ten thousand years of effort to perfect, it included something of the seaman's mind and heart that can neither be defined nor measured. He has paid and the story of the carrier is now the record of a great adventure organised into the commonplace, a breathtaking gamble that became a carefully calculated certainty run on facts and figures instead of dreams.

Bibliography

ANDERSON, John: *The Last Survivors in Sail*. 3rd rev. ed. London, 1948

BONE, David W.: *The Brassbounder*. London, 1910.

BOWEN, Frank C.: *From Carrack to Clipper*. 2nd rev. ed. London and New York, 1948

BROWN, A. J.: *Introduction to the World Economy*. London and New York, 1959

CARR, Frank G. G.: *The Cutty Sark and the Days of Sail*. London, n.d.

CONDLIFFE, J. B.: *The Commerce of Nations*. New York, 1950; London, 1951

CONRAD, Joseph: *The Mirror of the Sea*. London (Nelson Classics), 1958; New York (Doubleday, Anchor Books), 1960

CUNNINGHAM, W.: *The Growth of English Industry and Commerce during the Early and Middle Ages*. 5th ed. Cambridge, 1910; New York, 1967

DANA, Richard Henry: *Two Years before the Mast*. London, 1841; New York (Dial), n.d.

DOWNIE, W. I.: *Reminiscences of a Blackwall Midshipman*. London, 1912

FOSTER, Wm.: *The East India House*. London, 1924

GIBB, D. E. W.: *Lloyd's of London*. London, 1957; New York (St Martin's), n.d.

GREEN, J. R.: *A Short History of the English People*. London, 1874; New York (Dutton), n.d.

HAKLUYT, Richard: *Voyages*. London, Everyman ed. (Dent), 1906–; New York (Viking), 1965

LIPSON, E.: *A Short History of Wool*. London, New York, and Melbourne, 1953

LUBBOCK, Basil:

The Arctic Whalers. Glasgow, 1937

The Blackwall Frigates. 2nd ed. Glasgow, 1950

The China Clippers. 4th ed. Glasgow, 1919

The Down Easters. Glasgow, 1929

The Opium Clippers. Glasgow, 1933

The Last of the Windjammers. Glasgow, 1927

MORSE, H. B.: *The Chronicles of the East India Company*. Oxford, 1926–9; New York (Paragon), n.d.

MORTON, A. L.: *A People's History of England*. London, 1938; New York (International Publishers), n.d.

PEPYS, Samuel: *Diaries*. London, Everyman ed. (Dent), 1906–; New York (Random House), 1946

PIDDINGTON, H.: *The Sailor's Horn Book*. 6th ed. London, 1876

POPE-HENNESSY, James: *Sins of the Fathers*. London, 1967; New York, 1968

REED, T.: *Reed's Seamanship*, compiled and illustrated by W. Moore. 30th ed. Sunderland, 1952

REID, C. Lestock: *Commerce and Conquest*. London, 1947

ROSE, J. Holland: *Man and The Sea*. Cambridge, 1935

ROSE, Millicent: *The East End of London*. London, 1951

SCHLOTE, Werner: *British Overseas Trade from 1700 to the 1930s*, translated by W. O. Henderson and W. H. Chaloner. Oxford, 1952; New York (Macmillan), n.d.

SCOTT, M.: *Tom Cringle's Log*, with introduction by Mowbray Norrie. London, 1895

SELIGMAN, Adrian: *The Voyage of the Cap Pilar*. 2nd ed. London, 1951; New York (Dutton), n.d.

TAWNEY, R. H.: *English Economic History, Select Documents*. London, 1914

TREVELYAN, G. M.: *British History in the 19th Century*. 2nd ed. London, 1937; New York (Harper and Row), n.d.

WRIGHT, C., and FAYLE, C. Ernest: *History of Lloyd's*. London, 1928

Acknowledgements

THE AUTHOR AND PUBLISHERS wish to record their grateful thanks to copyright owners for the use of illustrations listed below:

Bibliothèque Nationale, Paris: 6, 20, 29
The Bristol Museum: 12
Calendars of Distinction: frontispiece
Cayzer Irvine and Co. Ltd: 58, 61
Cunard Steamship Co. Ltd: 40, 44
The Cutty Sark and the Days of Sail, by Frank G. Carr: 55
Laurence Dunn: 66
Gulf Oil (Great Britain) Ltd: 63
The Hull Museum: 15, 18
Library of Congress, Washington, D.C.: 59
Lloyd's: 21, 22
Lloyd's Register of Shipping: 23
The Mansell Collection: 13, 52, 57
Musée de Châteauroux and Monsieur Hubert de Lesseps: 45
The National Maritime Museum, Greenwich, London: 3, 5, 7, 14, 17, 24, 26, 28, 43, 47, 48, 49, 50, 51, 69
The National Portrait Gallery, London: 4, 16, 27
Overseas Containers Ltd: 69
Radio Times Hulton Picture Library: 1, 2, 19, 31, 53
The Science Museum, London: 25, 30, 32, 33, 34, 35, 36, 37, 38, 39, 41, 42, 62, 64, 65
Spink and Son Ltd: 8

The Tate Gallery, London: 46
The Wilberforce Museum, Kingston upon Hull: 10, 11
Yachting World: title-page

and for quotations:

George Allen and Unwin Ltd and W. W. Norton Company Inc. for J. B. Condliffe: *The Commerce of Nations*
Brown, Son and Ferguson, Ltd for Basil Lubbock: *The Arctic Whalers, The Blackwall Frigates, The China Clippers, The Last of the Windjammers*
The Clarendon Press for H. B. Morse: *The Chronicles of the East India Company*
The Cresset Press Ltd for Millicent Rose: *The East End of London*
W. Heffer and Sons Ltd for J. Holland Rose: *Man and the Sea*
Laurence and Wishart Ltd for A. L. Morton: *A People's History of England*
Macmillan and Co. Ltd for C. Wright and C. Ernest Fayle: *A History of Lloyds*
George Weidenfeld and Nicolson Ltd and Alfred A. Knopf Inc. for James Pope-Hennessy: *Sins of the Fathers*

Index

Printed in Great Britain by Jarrold and Sons Ltd., Norwich